19.23

THE SUITE LIFE

THE SUITE LIFE

THE
MAGIC AND MYSTERY
OF
HOTEL LIVING

CHRISTOPHER HEARD

DUNDURN
TORONTO

Editor: Michael Carroll
Design: Jesse Hooper
Printer: Marquis

Library and Archives Canada Cataloguing in Publication

Heard, Christopher
The suite life : the magic and mystery of hotel living / Christopher Heard.

ISBN 978-1-55488-862-7

1. Hotels. 2. Celebrities--Homes and haunts. I. Title.

TX911.2.H42 2011   647.94   C2010-907737-7

1   2   3   4   5   15   14   13   12   11

   Conseil des Arts   Canada Council   Canada      ONTARIO ARTS COUNCIL
du Canada   for the Arts   CONSEIL DES ARTS DE L'ONTARIO

We acknowledge the support of the **Canada Council for the Arts** and the **Ontario Arts Council** for our publishing program. We also acknowledge the financial support of the **Government of Canada** through the **Canada Book Fund** and **Livres Canada Books**, and the **Government of Ontario** through the **Ontario Book Publishing Tax Credit** and the **Ontario Media Development Corporation**.

Care has been taken to trace the ownership of copyright material used in this book. The author and the publisher welcome any information enabling them to rectify any references or credits in subsequent editions.

J. Kirk Howard, President

Printed and bound in Canada.
www.dundurn.com

SEP 1 6 2011

Dundurn   Gazelle Book Services Limited   Dundurn
3 Church Street, Suite 500   White Cross Mills   2250 Military Road
Toronto, Ontario, Canada   High Town, Lancaster, England   Tonawanda, NY
M5E 1M2   LA1 4XS   U.S.A. 14150

For my beautiful daughter, Princess Isabelle, as always

CONTENTS

ACKNOWLEDGEMENTS

Many thanks to the fine people at Dundurn Press, particularly president and publisher Kirk Howard and vice-president of marketing and sales Beth Bruder, who was my first contact at Dundurn. I will be forever grateful for their interest and support. I would also like to thank associate publisher and editorial director Michael Carroll, a calm and supportive editor who made this book better; director of sales and marketing Margaret Bryant; and designers Courtney Horner and Jesse Hooper. From that first lunch at the Scotland Yard pub on The Esplanade, I was instantly at ease with everyone at Dundurn. I knew *The Suite Life* was in the hands of the right publisher because the company embraced it not just as a book project but understood the whole spirit of it, as well.

Deep, heartfelt thanks go out to my wonderful Fairmont Royal York family — without you none of this would have been possible, not just the book but the very dream itself. So thanks to Fairmont regional vice-president and Royal York general manager Heather McCrory, whose early encouraging words on this material were very meaningful, in fact, crucial, to the process; to my good friend Mike Taylor, public relations director of Fairmont, who first uttered those three magical words — "writer-in-residence"; to Melanie Coates, who is everything from my sounding board to my guardian angel; to Kolene Elliott, who is one of the smartest and most resourceful hotel people I've ever encountered; to Serge Laroche, whose patience and understanding made a world of difference; to the very good people in the Fairmont Royal York Health Club — Jeannie Gallant, Alison, Soaria, Will, and especially Josh Stone, my good friend whom I bounced off whatever I was working on for his reaction. Anyone who loves *All in the Family* as much as I do is a wit I can trust without hesitation. Every single day during the researching and writing of this book began with Josh, and I thank him for his friendship and support. And, finally, thanks to the maids who work the ninth floor of the Royal York — you take such great care of me!

Thanks always to my family, father Bill Heard, mother Marie Heard, and brother Peter Heard.

Special thanks to the beautiful Rhonda Thain. For three books now (and counting), your love and support and comforting touch were extremely meaningful to me. I only hope a little of those things flowed back to you from me during these busy days.

Thanks also to my friend and fellow author Michael Coren for all his encouragement and support (and promotion).

Thanks to Ann Layton of Siren Communications, my fellow hotel lover and good friend. Many of the hotels described in this book I experienced because of you.

Special loving thanks to my beautiful little girl, Isabelle. It was through her inspiration that I was able to see this wonderful place and this magnificent experience as the magical dream come true living and writing this book really was.

And thanks to the griffin on the northeast corner of the Royal York for keeping an eye on me by day and by night.

INTRODUCTION

I HAVE ALWAYS ASSOCIATED HOTEL living with excitement and adventure, with romance and sensuality, with mystery and the sense that within the walls of a hotel everything is possible, anything can happen, and usually does. I link hotels with all the fascinating people I have met because more often than not the encounter was in a hotel. But the idea, the dream of living that life myself, was first inspired when I was 12 years old. Always a voracious reader, I read anything that caught my fancy whether I fully knew the reason for my interest or not. It was at that age that I was reading a book on the eccentric billionaire Howard Hughes, about how for many of the final years of his life he resided on the penthouse floors of fine hotels in Acapulco, Mexico, and Vancouver, British Columbia. Hughes was said to have lived in complete seclusion, even though he was in a place where thousands of people came and went on a weekly basis. The mysteriousness of that intrigued me, and as a young boy who was painfully shy and woefully introverted, the very notion of being a part of the world, being in the middle of a swirling microcosm of activity, while at the same time being able to shut oneself away from the hustle and bustle at will, intrigued the hell out of me and still, obviously, does.

My deeply rooted love affair with Toronto's Fairmont Royal York Hotel also began when I was very young. My mother, Marie, would bring my brother, Peter, and me to the Royal York for weekends from our home 35 miles east of the city. We would come in on Friday evenings, see a stage show or a movie or go to a museum, and walk the streets and eat in little restaurants and shop in huge bookstores. Then, on Sunday afternoons, we would return home. What I noticed about those Royal York weekends was that time appeared to elongate. Two full days at the hotel seemed to feel like a month, with each moment being savoured and enjoyed. Later I came to understand that I had an even deeper connection to the Royal York, but more about that later.

My lifelong attraction to movie history and culture, something I made a career out of, was also significantly intensified in the Royal York during one of my many childhood sojourns there. On one such occasion my mother was out with a friend for the evening and my younger brother was fast asleep in the suite. I was clicking around the TV channels and came across the in-room pay-per-view channels. I noticed that the acclaimed movies *Taxi Driver* and *One Flew over the Cuckoo's Nest* were a mere click away. I was too young to see the films on the big screen due to ratings restrictions, but here they were. I ordered both movies and was mesmerized by their stark realism, the brilliance of their screenplays, and the flawless, indelible performances of actors Robert De Niro and Jack Nicholson, their stars. I took in both films twice and came away thinking about movies in a whole new way — that they could thrill and entertain but could also dig deeply into the human condition.

Years later I told that story to Robert De Niro and to *One Flew over the Cuckoo's Nest* producer Saul Zaentz at different times during interviews, both sessions taking place in hotel suites (The Regency in New York City). In preparation for this book I did some rough calculations and determined that I've done more than 700 interviews in hotel suites, with a few of the most memorable ones in the Royal York. But the true magic of the Royal York really hit me one sunny afternoon in August.

My beautiful little daughter, Isabelle, was visiting me at the Royal York from her home in Windsor, Ontario, when she was three years old. Isabelle is smart, curious, creative, and energetic. She loves the Royal York and runs in the big, open spaces on the mezzanine level. I follow her around with a video camera so we can make our own little Eloise movies. On that particular Saturday afternoon we were in the lobby, and Isabelle was climbing the stairs leading to the venerable Imperial Room's large, ornate doors. They were closed, and nothing was happening in the Imperial Room that afternoon.

(Courtesy Fairmont Hotels & Resorts)

The Royal York Hotel's Imperial Room has showcased performances by Ella Fitzgerald and Louis Armstrong as well as by Tina Turner and my daughter, Isabelle.

Isabelle asked me, "What's in there?" I told her we could peek inside and have a look. We did so and saw the chandeliers and huge, draped windows. I heard a little "Wow" come from knee level. We slipped inside to look around. Isabelle was dazzled by the room's size, her attention drawn to the velvet curtains on the stage. I told her that singers and musicians once played on that stage and that all the empty tables we saw had been filled with people watching. She asked me if I could lift her onto the stage, and when she was up there, I sat at one of the circular tables directly in front. Isabelle danced and twirled and sang on the enormous stage.

As she performed, I envisioned the stars who had graced that stage over the past several decades — everyone from Peggy Lee and Tony Bennett to Marlene Dietrich and Ella Fitzgerald. I was sitting at a table where many a dandy had sat with his date taking in a show over drinks. Glancing around the room, I marvelled at how much history, how many stories, were contained in this place. Up on that stage, with the lingering spirit of Dietrich perhaps in attendance, my beautiful little girl was making her stage debut all by herself to the proudest and most enthusiastically supportive audience imaginable — her daddy.

Isabelle bounced across the stage, singing one of our favourite songs from the movie version of *The Cat in the Hat* — "He's a cat in a hat, he's a *chat* in a *chapeau*, he's a *gato* in a sombrero ..." The more she twirled the more energy she seemed to have. It was as if Peggy Lee were silently telling her to "Sing, Isabelle, sing." When she finally wore herself out and collapsed onto the stage laughing with red cheeks and an exaggerated show of being out of breath, she called to me that it was "Spaghetti time!" That meant lunch at the nearby Old Spaghetti Factory.

Outside, as we strolled along Front Street toward The Esplanade, Isabelle peered back at the Royal York. (The farther away you get the more immense and regal the old hotel looks). She smiled and asked me if the building was a "magical castle." I bent down to take in the view she was seeing and said, "Yes, Isabelle, it is."

BOOK ONE

A PRIVATE OASIS
OF
SOLITUDE
... WITH ROOM SERVICE

My FASCINATION WITH HOTELS, hotel living, and hotel culture began probably subconsciously when I heard my grandmother and grandfather (Annie and Raoul Godin) talk about the years they worked in a magical-sounding place called the Royal York Hotel. Life in this magic castle seemed unlike that of anywhere else, as if there was the life that swirled outside the doors and the life that had a different, dreamlike quality inside. Then later, when I began actually visiting the Royal York for weekend city excursions, I got a taste of the atmosphere first hand. We all know that life has a certain feel and that dreams have a quality of their own. Being in the Royal York was somewhere in between — better than one but not as fleeting as the other.

The allure of the Royal York never seemed to wane for me. For my 18th birthday my parents treated me to a weekend at the hotel for me and my best friend to tear up the town for three days by ourselves. It was the first time I checked into the Royal York by myself. I remember that weekend as a time of bookstores and fast food and hanging around in the suite watching movies and enjoying the place. When I checked out, the desk person said, "I hope we see you back here soon."

Even then I experienced the magnetism of the hotel, so I told her, "Oh, I'll most certainly see you all again … and often!"

My love for hotels really ramped up when I started staying in many of the finest ones in the world to interview movie stars for television. I got to know hotels well, to appreciate what they felt like, and to understand what made great ones great and what made mediocre ones always chase but never attain that greatness. I rubbed shoulders with people who had accomplished what I was dreaming of doing — actually living in a hotel. I could now ask the celebrities, the hotel managers, and sometimes the hotel owners about the magic of hotels.

By natural extension, because I was always a writer first and a TV guy second, I began writing about hotels and hotel living for various newspapers and magazines. Travel editors and hoteliers alike loved my take on hotels because I wasn't functioning as a hotel critic but as a hotel lover who wrote about the experience, the atmosphere, and the rhythm, not the thread count of sheets. With each new hotel experience I lived and each new hotel story I was told, another fibre was added to the fabric of my desire and dream to live in a hotel. I always knew that one day, without knowing when or under what circumstances, I was destined to fulfill my fantasy. Like Goethe once said, "Be bold and mighty forces will come to your aid."

In the introduction I mentioned that one of the initial sparks of inspiration that led to this book was reading about Howard Hughes and his long-time love affair with hotels. However, the billionaire's fascination didn't emerge in the last years of his life, as many believe, when he completely surrendered to his obsessions and compulsions. No, it actually began much earlier when Hughes hit Hollywood and became a director, producer, and mogul of sorts. He had a particular fondness for the renowned Beverly Hills Hotel, especially its famed pink stucco bungalows. In 1942 Hughes kept three or four bungalows on permanent reservation. He occupied one while his women, most often among them actress Jean Peters, had another. When Hughes was in residence at the Beverly Hills Hotel, the kitchen staff were told they should immediately make room for Hughes's personal chef when he needed to use the kitchen. Apparently, Howard's chef knew how to make his favourite pineapple upside-down cake, a duty the tycoon didn't entrust to anyone else.

It wasn't until the early to mid-1960s that Hughes, who had descended rapidly into a dark world of obsessive-compulsive disorders and paranoia, surrounded himself with Mormons as his aides and assistants. (Hughes believed Mormons could be trusted, since they were committed to a religious life and

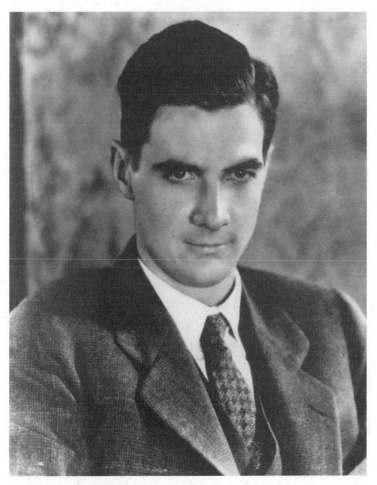

Billionaire Howard Hughes (1905–1976) was possibly the most eccentric long-time hotel resident who ever lived.

didn't drink, use drugs, or gamble.) He began to live permanently in one hotel after another, usually taking up an entire penthouse floor for himself and booking another entire lower floor to house his staff. In the 1960s, Hughes still operated his businesses, and when he embarked on his major hotel living phase, he had just been issued the largest personal cheque in U.S. history ($566 million) after selling Trans World Airlines (TWA).

The action in Las Vegas around that time was really heating up. The city was starting to seem like the new Hollywood, or at least Tinseltown's looser and wilder sister. Hughes and his Mormon army headed to Las Vegas and the Desert Inn (which was demolished in 2002 to make way for the Wynn Las Vegas Resort and Casino that stands in its place today), but the welcome wasn't exactly warm and open-armed. The owner of the Desert Inn was a Las Vegas swashbuckler named Barney "Moe" Dalitz, who had been a friend of another Vegas buccaneer (actually, a stone-cold killer) named Benjamin "Bugsy" Siegel, who had built the Flamingo Hotel with Mafia money and was murdered by his gangster pals when the return on their investment wasn't what he had promised. Dalitz was very concerned about Hughes and his Mormon squad taking up so much of his hotel, especially with Christmas and the lucrative holiday season approaching. A deal was struck between Dalitz and Hughes. The billionaire could take over the top floor of the hotel for himself and one a few floors below for his staff, but they all had to be out on December 1. Hughes moved in and found it very much to his liking, so when December 1 came and went, he and his posse were still there.

Dalitz was beside himself with frustration. Hughes and Team Mormon were costing him money. With the holidays coming up, it was intolerable to have his hotel filled with

Mormons who didn't drink or gamble. Dalitz tried everything in his power to move Hughes out of the hotel, which really irritated the tycoon. So, flush with the TWA sale cash, Hughes simply bought the Desert Inn and moved Dalitz out. At the time this action was deemed very eccentric, but the best was yet to come. Once Hughes owned the hotel, he sealed of his floor from public access and had a security checkpoint mounted at the elevators to make sure no one tried to get onto his floor. He installed a movie screen and a projector with a full theatre sound system in his penthouse, and during his time there, he became obsessed with the Rock Hudson movie *Ice Station Zebra*. Hughes watched the film over and over at all hours of the night at full volume, causing other guests to complain that their windows were rattling and that booming sounds were disturbing their sleep.

Next door to the Desert Inn at the time was another hotel called the Silver Slipper, which boasted a giant neon slipper sign out front. Hughes became obsessed with that giant neon slipper so close to his hotel. He was afraid it was too big and would one day collapse and fall onto his hotel, so he bought the Silver Slipper in order to do something about the sign. Hughes went on to purchase four Las Vegas hotels and casinos before he was through, often simply because he *could*, not for any rational investment purpose.

Howard Hughes was now a creature of whim but on a grand scale. When he tired of Las Vegas, he went on an eccentric world tour of hotel living that took him and his Mormon crew first to Britannia Beach Hotel on the Bahamas' Paradise Island. However, the stay there wasn't as long as Hughes desired because of visa problems with a number of his entourage. It was underreported how many people were in the group, causing Bahamian authorities to raise questions.

Rather than go through any kind of scrutiny, Hughes simply selected another hotel and moved on.

The billionaire next set his sights on Canada, but his original idea of relocating at the Queen Elizabeth Hotel in Montreal soured when John Lennon and Yoko Ono moved in and wrote and recorded their iconic anti-war anthem "Give Peace a Chance" during their famous bed-in. Ideologically, that scene didn't sit well with Hughes, since Hughes Aircraft made huge profits supplying the U.S. armed forces with planes and helicopters for use in the Vietnam War.

Hughes settled on Vancouver, British Columbia, and took over a good portion of the Bayshore Hotel at the entrance to Stanley Park. From there Hughes and his team headed to the Ritz-Carlton in Boston on the edge of Boston Common. Hughes was in Boston to establish a medical centre in his name because he believed all the best medical minds were currently in that city. Once that was done, Hughes returned to the Beverly Hills Hotel because he needed to conclude some business, including details surrounding his impending divorce from Jean Peters. When that was accomplished, the Hughes team flew to Acapulco. Hughes took up residence on the penthouse floor of the Fairmont Princess Hotel, where John Wayne and Lana Turner had also lived for a while.

While in Mexico, Hughes, an avid and voracious reader, got it into his head that the next emerging place worthy of investing in was Nicaragua. He agreed with what President Anastasio Somoza was doing in the region and liked that the United States had friendly relations with the country. So he and his squad moved to the splendid Inter-Continental near Lake Managua in Nicaragua, a beautiful structure built to resemble a pre-Colombian temple. In December 1972, while Hughes and his entourage were in Managua, a 6.5-magnitude earthquake rocked the region and did extensive damage to the city. Somoza instantly had Hughes and his people moved into a wing of his presidential palace until he could arrange to relocate (and so Hughes would still consider investing in his country). Within a few days Hughes and his Mormons were on their way to the Xanadu Princess Hotel in Freeport in the Bahamas, and yes, he did buy that hotel, as well, before moving in.

The Xanadu Princess was the last hotel Hughes lived in. He died a few years later on April 5, 1976. The details of his demise are sketchy at best. He lived his life so reclusively, so mysteriously, that the circumstances of his death can only be narrowed to two scenarios. One is that he was flying from his penthouse at the Fairmont Princess in Acapulco to the Methodist Hospital in Houston, Texas, for treatment of a kidney ailment. The other scenario has him dying while headed back to his home in the Xanadu Princess in Freeport from Houston after treatment for a kidney ailment.

A number of Hughes's biographers have speculated on why Hughes chose to reside in hotels for many years. The general consensus comes down to his desire to live in a controlled, convenient environment where he could be in absolute seclusion if he wished but still be surrounded by a support structure that was always there and could always be counted on.

Another person I met who had an interest in Howard Hughes and was a long-time hotel resident was actor/filmmaker Warren Beatty, who tried for years to make a movie about Hughes but could never quite pull it together. For just over ten years Beatty chose to live in the old, iconic Beverly Wilshire Hotel that is almost right across the street from Rodeo Drive in Beverly

Hills. The actor was at loose ends in the early to mid-1960s, he was a Hollywood Lothario more famous for who he was dating than as an actor, he had been in a string of flops, and he had a bad reputation among directors and producers in town. Then a script landed in his lap, and he thought the best way to get it done was to produce it himself. The problem with his scheme, though, was that it was still the time of the studio system. To make a film at Warner Bros., for instance, you had to get the approval of Jack Warner himself. Actors usually didn't produce movies, especially pretty-boy ones.

Beatty returned from Europe where he had been shooting on location. He didn't have a place to live, so he checked into the Beverly Wilshire Hotel in a suite on the penthouse floor. However, his suite wasn't as grandiose as the penthouse might indicate. He had a two-room suite, a large living room, and a bedroom divided with sliding French doors. What made the penthouse floor attractive was that the suites came with a large terrace off both the bedroom and the living room. Beatty checked into the hotel because it was a favourite haunt of his. (The Boulevard Restaurant and Boulevard Lounge were great spots to be seen having meetings in the old Hollywood.) It wasn't his initial intention to remain there for more than ten years, but the comfort and the convenience became something he grew used to very quickly. "I can say I didn't intend to live in the hotel that long, but since I wasn't really actively thinking of an alternative, I must have been just fine with the arrangement," Beatty told me. He lived in the Beverly Wilshire from age 28 through 39.

On May 9, 1998, I sat down with Beatty in a huge suite in the Four Seasons Hotel in Beverly Hills. It was one of those warm, fragrant Southern California days that capture the very essence of why so many people drift out there and never leave.

The interview was being shot for television, so Beatty asked for a good deal of control as to how it would be staged. He wasn't comfortable doing television interviews, but he was proud of his most recent film, the political satire *Bulworth*, and was prepared to bite this particular bullet. When I entered the suite, he worked with the lighting people to arrange how the room was lit. The illumination was quite soft and gave him an almost gauzy look on screen. Beatty was still a handsome man, so I thought the vanity lighting was unnecessary. He was comfortably dressed in corduroy pants and a thin sweater and seemed extraordinarily talkative, especially when the subject of hotels came up. I mentioned my fascination for hotels to him and asked him about his experiences living in one.

"I had been living in hotels on and off for years, anyway," Beatty said. "That's the kind of transient, transitory life of an actor, so when you're doing that kind of work, it isn't a matter of liking or not liking hotel living. It's almost a necessity." But transient and transitory, I suggested, didn't define a place you choose to live for more than a decade. "No, but that wasn't the intention when I first moved into the Beverly Wilshire. I wanted a good central location to stay for a while during a time I was going through some career re-evaluation and adjustment. Then a month became two, two became six, a year became three ..."

When I asked Beatty what was the one thing that sprang to mind about living in a hotel that made it something he elected to do rather than something he was forced to do out of work necessity, he said, "It's very convenient and it's very simple. Those two things are actually one in the same. When you live a simple, uncluttered existence, you gain a kind of personal freedom that's very convenient. Living in a hotel removes many little decisions and choices in the day, and once you get used to not having to make all those little decisions, you don't even think about them anymore and you have that much more time to do the things you're trying to get done."

During Beatty's time in the Beverly Wilshire, he instructed the front desk to allow calls through to his suite without screening them first, since he loved talking on the phone. Those who visited his suite, such as his long-time friend and collaborator screenwriter Robert Towne, described the suite as "full of books and scripts and magazines." Towne also told me: "Warren would always have at least one room service tray in the room. He would order room service, then forget to call down to have them pick up the tray, as he would be off on another phone call or get caught up in another meeting. Not that the space was messy. It wasn't at all. It was all very ordered and arranged and neat, but you could look around the suite and get a pretty good picture of what kinds of things interested him and what kinds of things didn't."

After the enormous critical and financial success of *Bonnie and Clyde*, Beatty's Beverly Wilshire suite became a busy hub of activity, meetings, and conferences all day. Romantic encounters abounded. The Beverly Wilshire became known partly as the place where Warren Beatty lived. Beautiful women seen in the lobby were naturally assumed to be on their way up to the penthouse, and because Beatty made the rare arrangement with the front desk that his calls be relayed directly to his room without screening, the hotel had no idea which women were invited by prior arrangement by Beatty and which were trying to catch his fancy, something that ultimately made living in the Beverly Wilshire quite inconvenient for him.

Beatty left the Beverly Wilshire in the early 1970s around the time he was making *Shampoo*. By that time he had been in the hotel for almost ten years, his star had grown much brighter, and his reputation had become far more dynamic. Because Beatty's lifestyle was a kind of love 'em and leave 'em one, there were more than a few disgruntled women, husbands, and boyfriends out there. And, of course, everyone knew he lived in the Beverly Wilshire. Beatty was made even more uncomfortable when the Beverly Wilshire built an addition that looked down on Beatty's once-secluded terrace.

But let's get back to the connection between Howard Hughes and Warren Beatty. When I asked Beatty where his interest in Hughes came from, he told me he had been actively trying to develop a major film based on the later years of the billionaire. The actor could have certainly pulled off the feat. The movie he did after *Shampoo*, *The Fortune*, featured him styled to look like Hughes, slicked-back hair, thin moustache, and all. In this role he resembled a slightly more handsome version of the real Hughes.

Beatty told me he had purchased a house on Mulholland Drive in the hills above Sunset Boulevard (nicknamed then Bad Boy Drive because Beatty's new neighbours were Jack Nicholson and Marlon Brando) but seemed in no hurry to occupy the house. After he left the Beverly Wilshire, he moved into the Beverly Hills Hotel where he worked day after day with writer Robert Towne and director Hal Ashby on the *Shampoo* screenplay. One night Beatty noticed two big guys in black suits at the end of his hallway as he returned to his suite. Then he noticed another two equally stern-looking black-suited dudes at the opposite end of the hallway. Once in his suite, the over-sensitive, borderline paranoid Beatty called down to the front desk and demanded to know who the guys were in the hallway. Clearly, they were bodyguards of one sort or another. The man at the desk explained that he wasn't allowed to divulge that kind of information, even though he was aware he was speaking to Warren Beatty.

Not someone to be denied anything, Beatty persisted and wore down the desk attendant in short order. The man explained that these fellows were Mormon bodyguards for Howard Hughes. Beatty peppered the desk attendant with questions, starting with "Is Hughes in the suite next to mine?"

"Who knows?" the desk clerk said.

Hughes had reserved six suites and was in one of them, but not even the staff knew which one. Beatty then asked the desk attendant why Hughes didn't take the secluded bungalows the hotel offered.

"Well," replied the desk attendant, "Mr. Hughes actually does have four of the bungalows set aside, as well."

Beatty asked why they were kept empty.

The deskman said, "Oh, they aren't empty, Mr. Beatty. The bungalows are where Mr. Hughes keeps his women."

It hardly seems coincidental that it was around this time that Warren Beatty began to develop his own ideas of one day playing the legendary billionaire on the screen.

There is a spot in Los Angeles that is home to actor James Woods and has been for the past four years. The hotel is called L'Ermitage, or more accurately Raffles L'Ermitage (*ermitage* is French for "retreat"). Having stayed at Raffles L'Ermitage a number of times myself, I can fully attest to its luxury. The hotel was built in the 1970s as a high-end condo. Because of its proximity to the shopping on Rodeo Drive and to Sunset Boulevard in the other direction, the location is perfect. Thanks to the configurations of the layout when Raffles L'Ermitage was a condo, the standard rooms are actually quite large (over 675 square feet per standard room). The name of this hotel is appropriate, since unless you know exactly where you're going, you'll miss it. And that's precisely why both Michael Jackson and Elizabeth Taylor chose the place to recover quietly from cosmetic surgery.

I first met Woods at L'Ermitage before he was living there and before I was residing in the Royal York. My objective was to interview him about a role in *Where the Boys Are*, a movie he was starring in opposite Drew Barrymore. I was in a nice suite overlooking the Hollywood Hills; he was in a larger suite where we set up our on-camera interview. As we got ready, we chatted about our love of cool hotels and about the hotel we were in. We talked about our mutual wish one day to live in a hotel, and it was funny that while Woods was still a few years away from moving into L'Ermitage, he looked around the suite and said, "This might not be such a bad choice right here."

Jump ahead six years. I was back in Los Angeles at L'Ermitage and once again speaking to James Woods, only by now he had actually been living in the hotel for more than a year. Of course, living in the hotel was our first order of business for conversation. "I was having problems with my house," Woods told me, "structural things that needed work, some repairs. The house was in need of some substantial renovations and repairs. I had an estimate done and found that it was going to cost almost what the house cost all over again, so I just got rid of the house and moved in here with the intention of staying until I decided where I wanted to live next. But after a few weeks, then a few months, it kind of dawned on me that I loved living here, that this was where I wanted to live next."

I pressed Woods on the pros and cons of choosing the life of a hotel liver, and he said, "Well, it can get a bit pricey in a place like this, but you balance it off with the added comfort and the significant convenience, and it becomes something that can be quite reasonably justified." Woods spoke about the little things you grow used to when you live in a hotel. "One thing that is kind of nice is that I can ask one of the guys [bellmen] here to take my dog for a walk, and he happily does it. I'm not using the guy as a slave. It's like he's a pal doing another pal a favour. You can always count on that pal to do you that favour when needed. I bought the main guy a very nice set of golf clubs as a way of thanking him for always being there when I need him."

Other than my beloved Royal York in Toronto, perhaps my favourite hotel in the world is Chateau Marmont, located in the eight thousand block of Sunset Boulevard in West Hollywood. That venerable place is as much a part of Hollywood as the Academy Awards and is one of the few hotels in the world that wears its notoriety like a badge of honour. Construction on Chateau Marmont began in 1927, and it opened for business two years later. California attorney Fred Horowitz built the hotel after being inspired by the Château d'Amboise in the Loire Valley in France. The hotel is tucked away off Sunset Boulevard and is accessible only by a steep, winding driveway. (Celebrity photographer Helmut Newton died when he lost control of his car on this serpentine driveway and crashed into the high wall beside it.) Horowitz made sure, to his brilliant foresight, that the hotel was erected well above the contemporary standards for earthquake-proofing, and because of that the hotel survived major earthquakes in 1933, 1953, 1971, 1987, and 1994. (I was actually in Chateau Marmont during the 1994 tremors, my first such experience with an earthquake. As instructed, I stood in the doorframe until the swaying and rumbling stopped, then West Hollywood went immediately back to being cool and laid-back.)

Chateau Marmont consists of a main building with standard rooms, larger suites, and penthouse suites with big terraces that overlook Sunset Boulevard and Beverly Hills. There are also four bungalows in the garden by the swimming pool. Strangely, to the discerning hotel person, Chateau Marmont is actually quite grungy on the surface, but that's also a major part of its charm and a chief reason why Hollywood actors and musicians are drawn to the place. In 1990, when the high-flying New York hotelier André Balazs bought Chateau Marmont, he announced he was going to upgrade the establishment but quickly reversed himself when many of the better-known patrons of the hotel objected. They told him that if he messed with the hotel and diminished its charm and atmosphere, they would find a new spot to play in. Balazs did do some minor work and upgrades on the hotel, but they were done so that most people hardly noticed them.

Chateau Marmont in West Hollywood is one of the most famous celebrity hotels, having been the site of Marilyn Monroe's suicide and John Belushi's drug overdose death.

Movie mogul Harry Cohn once said to his new star actors William Holden and Glenn Ford, "If you're going to get caught doing something indiscreet, make sure you get caught doing it at Chateau Marmont." Before taking up residence in the Beverly Hills Hotel, Howard Hughes moved into the attic at Chateau Marmont because it overlooked the swimming pool. He would survey the pool with powerful binoculars, searching for beautiful starlets whom he would then have an assistant summon for him.

When F. Scott Fitzgerald had pretty much come to the end of his productive years as a novelist, he went to Hollywood to accept lucrative writing gigs from the studios and chose to live at Chateau Marmont where he suffered a massive heart attack. Judy Garland was fond of sitting in the lounge off the reception area where there was a grand piano. She would play the piano and sing at the top of her lungs while the hotel staff went about their business around her.

Vivien Leigh resided in the hotel's suite 5D (at Chateau Marmont suites are assigned letters and numbers, the number indicating the floor, the letter the suite) after breaking up with her husband, Laurence Olivier. She was so traumatized by her estrangement that she had the entire living room area wallpapered top to bottom with photographs of the Shakespearean actor. However, in the bedroom of the suite there was just one picture of the two of them together that rested on the pillow beside where she slept.

In the 1950s, when bad-boy director Nicholas Ray lived in one of the bungalows at Chateau Marmont during the casting of his movie *Rebel Without a Cause*, a new young hothead actor named James Dean wanted to meet with him and talk about the film. Ray struck an intimidating figure — tall, black eye patch over one eye, gruff-voiced. He said he would meet Dean when he was good and ready. One night, while Ray was auditioning three actors — Natalie Wood, Dennis Hopper, and Sal Mineo — who made it into the legendary film, they were all startled by the commotion of the screen on one of the windows being ripped open. To their astonishment, Dean was crawling in through the window, demanding that he be allowed to audition for the role that eventually made him a celluloid icon. He fell into the bungalow onto a table that collapsed under him. Then he got to his feet and said that Ray had two choices: let him read or call the cops. Ray let him read.

A few years later, in 1956, another major heartthrob actor, Montgomery Clift, was in Los Angeles shooting a film called *Raintree County* with Elizabeth Taylor. One night, halfway through filming, Clift left a party at the home of Taylor and her then husband, Michael Wilding. His friend actor Kevin McCarthy was in another car ahead of Clift. The intoxicated Clift slammed his car into a telephone pole and was severely injured. His once-beautiful face was broken and mangled when it smashed against the steering wheel. McCarthy returned to Taylor's house to get help. When Taylor heard about the accident, she rushed to the scene, cradled Clift in his wrecked vehicle, and stopped him from choking on his broken teeth. The stricken actor was minutes away from dying when help arrived. After Clift was released from the hospital, Taylor arranged for him to move into Chateau Marmont for as long as he needed to recuperate.

In the 1960s, West Hollywood was abuzz with the changing music scene. Just down from Chateau Marmont is the legendary nightclub Whisky a Go-Go. It was in that club that Jim Morrison and The Doors broke out. And it was in Chateau Marmont where Jim Morrison claimed he had used up "eight of my nine lives." One of his most famous used-up lives occurred one evening when he was as high as a weather balloon and decided to take a shortcut from a rooftop terrace to his suite by leaping for a drainpipe and trying to swing into the window of his room. He barely made it and injured his back painfully in the process. Morrison used up life number nine in a hotel in Paris on July 3, 1971.

Chateau Marmont has seen tragedy as well as typical Hollywood antics. In 1982 comic actor John Belushi was living in one of the bungalows flush with the success of *Saturday Night Live* and his transition to movies, but he had also given in to the more self-indulgent aspects of Hollywood celebrity. Belushi was a well-known drug user and boozer whose intake of both grew daily. One warm night Belushi took his drug habit up a notch and injected himself with a lethal combination of heroin and cocaine that finally killed him. Another resident of the hotel and friend of Belushi, Robert De Niro, was so shocked by the comedian's death that it caused him to re-evaluate his own life and career. De Niro lived in one of Chateau Marmont's penthouse suites for two years.

Today Chateau Marmont is still a gathering place for hip Hollywood. The troubled actress Lindsay Lohan stayed there for a few years (2006 through 2008), and it was her preferred sanctuary after her drunk-driving arrest. One of Lohan's friends, Britney Spears, has the rare distinction of being barred a few times from Chateau Marmont for being unruly. When you're barred from Chateau Marmont for unruliness then it's a certainty you were being truly unruly.

The hotel continues to be featured in movies. Sofia Coppola, the daughter of Francis Ford Coppola, sets her 2010 film *Somewhere* in Chateau Marmont. In the movie Johnny Marco (Stephen Dorff) is a newly famous film star doing publicity for his latest flick while living in the hotel. Like many of his real-life counterparts, Johnny behaves badly in the hotel, drinking, drugging, and fornicating between bouts of driving around in his Ferrari and reacquainting himself with his preteen daughter, Cleo (Elle Fanning).

Actor Keanu Reeves, who doesn't own a home in Los Angeles, has lived in Chateau Marmont for years. He was photographed as late as February 2010 strolling out of the hotel, a place he finds comfortable, secluded, and familiar. Knowing that Reeves has resided in the hotel for a long time, I was curious about that part of his secretive life. I had a lengthy conversation with him in the Essex House Hotel in New York City where he was promoting *The Devil's Advocate*, a movie he did with Al Pacino. Between interviews we sat in an empty suite where Keanu wanted to watch some of the Dallas Cowboys' football games on TV. Outside of the formality of a structured on-camera Q and A we were free to chat about anything (except the movie he was promoting, of course; he was already tired of talking about that). We spoke about his youth in Toronto and how he skipped school to hang out in the pinball arcade in Union Station across Front Street from the Royal York.

I asked Reeves what it was about living in hotels that appealed to him. "After I started working in films regularly," he said, "it was a big part of that life. I would live in hotels while on location and then live in hotels in L.A. when I was between films because I seemed to be only there for a couple of months before having to head out on a location again. So it became what I'm used to pretty quickly. I'm heading to Australia soon to make a film, and I'll be there probably for the better part of a year."

Reeves said the difference between living in a secluded private residence in Los Angeles and the relative public nature of living in a hotel, especially given the fact that he is a private man, is: "There's a convenience and a simplicity and a lack of complication about living in a hotel, and there are layers of security that allow you to just withdraw into your space within the hotel and relax or do whatever you want with the confidence that you aren't going to be bothered." I then asked him why he chose Chateau Marmont as his hotel of choice. "I stayed there early on when I started getting some work, and it was just a very cool place to be. The building is old and rich with history, and the location of the place is pretty ideal. It's where a lot of meetings happen, and it's where a lot of other actors you end up knowing hang out. I really like it there. I find it very comfortable."

Hotels like Chateau Marmont are grungy almost by design. They straddle that fine line between grungy hip and plain grungy and do it in such a way that it becomes a selling point, a mythical energy that emanates outward and draws people there. Then there are other hotels that gain well-earned notoriety with no sense or plan of becoming part of a larger legend or myth and without any intention of making their fame a marketing strategy. One such hotel is the Chelsea in New York City. Situated at 222 West 23rd Street between 7th and 8th Avenues, the Chelsea has been a hub of New York's artistic, cultural, and bohemian activity for almost 130 years. When the Chelsea, a 12-storey red-brick structure, opened its doors in 1884, it was briefly the tallest building in Manhattan. The hotel was originally intended as the city's first-ever apartment co-operative. Back then Manhattan's Chelsea district was a bustling part of town, but when the theatres and other attractions relocated uptown, the co-operative went under. In 1905 the building reopened as the hotel it remains to this day.

One of the architectural delights of Hotel Chelsea is the ornate staircase that reaches from the ground floor all the way to the top floor, a staircase that isn't accessible to the public, only to registered guests. An early story of the Chelsea to make the papers the world over was when several of the survivors of the sinking of the *Titanic* were taken there to live because of the hotel's proximity to Pier 54 where they arrived.

The Chelsea became even more celebrated around the globe as a place where writers and artists not only lived but created some of the greatest works of art and literature of the modern age. This fact is something that interests me a lot, since it's been my experience that I've produced more work as a hotel resident than I ever did otherwise. The people and achievements associated with the Chelsea are too numerous to recount here. They would, in fact, make a book all by themselves and have done so a number of times, including in Ed Hamilton's excellent *Legends of the Chelsea Hotel: Living with the Legends and Outlaws of New York's Rebel Mecca.* The short list of highs and lows at the Chelsea includes Arthur C. Clarke writing his landmark novel *2001: A Space Odyssey* and Jack Kerouac penning his bohemian novel *On the Road.* Other authors who lived in the Chelsea are Mark Twain, Arthur Miller, Thomas Wolfe, and Jean-Paul Sartre. Charles R. Jackson wrote the novel *The Lost Weekend* while living in the Chelsea, then killed himself there. It is also a legend that poet Dylan Thomas died of alcohol poisoning in his suite at the Chelsea, but that isn't entirely true. He collapsed in his home at the Chelsea but didn't die until a few days later in a hospital.

Filmmakers Stanley Kubrick and Milos Forman also resided in the Chelsea, as did actor/director/author Ethan Hawke. When I spoke with Hawke about his sojourn at the Chelsea, he said, "I have never been so inspired by a place ever, and not inspired in any way that is conscious. I cannot say that because of this I was inspired to do that. The whole fucking place just seemed to be alive, literally alive, like you could feel it breathing and thinking." Hawke refers to the Chelsea in his novels *Ash Wednesday* and *The Hottest State*, and in 2002 he made a film called *Chelsea Walls*, which he directed and financed himself. It was shot on digital video and was a look at a day in the life of several artists living in the Chelsea at the same time.

Musicians who have called the Chelsea home are Edith Piaf, Bob Dylan, Janis Joplin, Jimi Hendrix, Leonard Cohen, and Sid Vicious of The Sex Pistols, who, on October 12, 1978, stabbed his girlfriend, Nancy Spungen, to death in their suite. Visual artists once in residence at the Chelsea include Frida Kahlo, Diego Rivera, Willem de Kooning, Robert Mapplethorpe, and many of Andy Warhol's crew. Warhol made a film in 1966 entitled *Chelsea Girls* about the female members of his so-called Factory who called the Chelsea home.

New York City's Hotel Chelsea is much loved by creative types as a short-term or long-term residence. Authors, artists, filmmakers, and musicians such as Mark Twain, Jean-Paul Sartre, Dylan Thomas, Robert Mapplethorpe, Diego Rivera, Milos Forman, Stanley Kubrick, Bob Dylan, Sid Vicious, and Edith Piaf have stayed here.

At present the Chelsea is still the residence of a number of long-term occupants, the longest of whom is Susanne Bartsch, a Swiss-born socialite who makes a living organizing and hosting outlandish New York nightlife parties. She has lived in the Chelsea for 20 years. Today the hotel has been refurbished into a respectable, almost upscale hotel. It wears its history proudly, but if you're coming to the Chelsea to stay where Jack Kerouac drank and feverishly wrote *On the Road*, then you'll be staying within the same walls, of course, but the place will be worlds away from the 1950s.

A trend I find curious arose in New York City in the late 1980s and early 1990s. Hoteliers bought up warehouses or office buildings and converted them into small hotels with a few rooms and rechristened them "boutique" hotels, even though they weren't that by classic definition. They were merely small hotels. In the swinging 1960s in London, England, the term *boutique hotel* came into existence to describe establishments that were smaller, catered to the hip crowd, and offered amenities the big hotels couldn't, such as addressing guests by their first names and providing particular needs ahead of being asked simply by knowing what those needs were. Now any hotel under 100 rooms receives the boutique label, even though they are nothing more than smaller versions of big hotels.

I spent some time in one such New York City "boutique" hotel that was considered super-chic and described itself as a seamless fusion of uptown luxury and downtown cool: the Chambers Hotel on Fifth Avenue just off 56th Street. Location-wise you couldn't ask for a better spot. The Chambers is steps away from the main shopping section of Fifth Avenue and a short stroll to Broadway and Times Square, but the suites seem to strain, groan, and stretch themselves into an approximation of ultra-cool so that you won't notice that the lobby is tiny, the lounge area is claustrophobic, and that what you can order to eat is extremely limited. The suite I was in had bare industrial concrete walls. The ceilings, too, were brutalist concrete, only they had exposed air duct tubing, as well. The bathroom had a modern rain shower but was quite tight and small. Notepaper on the desk was on a roll. You rolled it out onto the desk, made notes, then tore it off.

Of course, I understand the need to be unique and a little cooler than the guy down the block, but a hotel needs to consider one thing above all else — comfort. Every hotel guest I've ever questioned answers comfort when I ask what the first thing they expect from a hotel they've chosen. And while I'm not saying the Chambers Hotel doesn't have an atmosphere of New York hipster cool, I can only relate my personal experiences with it. Waking up that first morning there, I had the feeling I was secretly moved during the night from a hotel room to the boiler room in the basement.

In Canada the hotel landscape that resembles New York's the most is Montreal's. Both cities have a vast array of big old hotels with rich histories, brand-new modern versions of boutique hotels, and large convention-size chain hotels all functioning alongside one another by providing guests with what they need and expect. A Montreal establishment about the same size as the Chambers Hotel in New York is Hotel Godin at 10 Sherbrooke Street West. The chief difference between the Chambers and Hotel Godin is that the latter (which has the maiden name of my mother coincidentally) offers up minimalist cool, elegance, and chic but does so by enveloping its guests in shaded comfort. The walls are painted deep red, dark orange, and dark grey, and the rooms and suites have a high-tech look, but the beds and furniture are comfortable and cozy.

Hotel Godin was troubled since it opened in 2004. It never established a proper restaurant, which is essential in any hotel for it to be recommended over another hostelry. Because the hotel has a good location and because it was beautifully designed, it caught the eye of West Coast developer Trilogy Properties, which stepped in and transformed the place from the Godin into Opus Montreal. The first thing the new boss, John Evans, did was put in motion a multi-million-dollar plan to add a 1,800-square-foot restaurant as well as complete the never-finished terrace lounge and add an additional 500-square-foot bar separate from the restaurant. The scheme involved making the former Hotel Godin as close to what a real boutique operation should be.

In the 1950s, British-born but Canadian-raised author Arthur Hailey was a writer with the Canadian Broadcasting Corporation and got his first taste of success when he wrote a television drama called *Flight into Danger*, which was about a plane put into peril because of food poisoning. Paramount Pictures bought the rights to the drama and made a big-screen film entitled *Zero Hour*. (Decades later Paramount did a wildly funny spoof of the story with *Airplane!*) The story was so successful that Hailey was encouraged to write it as a novel. *Runway Zero-Eight* was published in 1958 and was well received. Hailey had found a new niche for his talents. He became known for tales that featured a multitude of diverse characters weaving in and out of one another's lives within the context of a single setting, industry, or profession. His next book, *The Final Diagnosis* (1959), was situated in a big-city hospital's pathology department. He followed that with *In High Places*, which has a backdrop of Cold War paranoia in North America. Then he turned his attention to the Royal York Hotel for his fourth novel, simply called *Hotel*.

Hailey had always been fascinated by the world within a world that hotels are and wanted to write a novel about what goes on in a suite juxtaposed against what transpires in the executive offices, the sort of things the general hotel guest would never imagine happening. He decided he wanted the setting for his novel to be a regal old hotel that had the distinction and colour of a long and storied history. Hailey needed a hotel that would be accessible to his audience. He didn't want a hotel like the Ritz in Paris or the Waldorf-Astoria in New York because they were too well-known and too luxurious. If he used a model like that, his story would become focused *on* the place, not set *in* the place, would become *about* the hotel and not so much about the people *in* the hotel. He had to live in a hotel before he wrote his novel and knew he would be fictionalizing the establishment for added literary freedom. Without much thinking or searching, he chose Toronto's Royal York.

The bestselling author's methodology when writing a book was to do at least a year of research, followed by six months or so of reviewing and digesting everything he had come up with, then another year to construct the novel from the ground up. His research stint living in the Royal York began in mid-1962 and continued almost to the end of 1963. During his time in the Royal York, he read almost 30 books on hotel administration and made a detailed survey of the hotel from top to bottom.

Arthur Hailey's Hotel *was a mammoth bestseller from the moment it first appeared in 1965.*

Hailey relocated his story from Toronto to New Orleans and renamed his hotel the St. Gregory, but every description in his book belongs to the Royal York. Knowing the Royal York as intimately as I do made for a strange experience when I first read *Hotel*. Hailey describes a character walking down the stairs, then out the ornate entranceway onto Corondelet Street. Well, I walk out those doors myself hundreds of times, and they don't lead to Corondelet Street in New Orleans but to Front Street in Toronto. As dense as the book is in terms of characters and the dramas they're involved in, the whole story plays out over five days. It has been suggested that Hailey based his novel not on the Royal York in Toronto but on the Roosevelt Hotel in New Orleans, another iconic hostelry that was coincidentally bought by the Fairmont chain in 1965, the year of the novel's publication, and renamed first the Fairmont Roosevelt and then later dubbed the Fairmont New Orleans. However, that supposition doesn't make sense, since Hailey did all his research while living in the Royal York.

Like many of Hailey's novels, *Hotel* was translated into a movie first and then a long-running TV series 16 years later (a testament to the popularity of the book and its subject matter). In 1967 Warner Bros. released the film version of *Hotel*, directed by Richard Quine. It was extremely faithful to the book and starred Rod Taylor, Merle Oberon, Michael Rennie, and my pal Karl Malden, who will turn up in this book again a little later and a lot more personally. On September 21, 1983, a television series based on Hailey's novel debuted. It was directed by Jerry London (*Shogun*), the king of the miniseries, and starred James Brolin, who was twice nominated for Golden Globe Awards for his work in the show, as was his female co-lead Connie Sellecca. The series, produced by Aaron Spelling, was a solid hit and ran for five seasons and 116 episodes. The St. Gregory Hotel in the television series was moved once again, this time from New Orleans to San Francisco. Much of the on-location work was done at the Fairmont San Francisco Hotel where to this day you can call down and have the pilot episode shown on your in-room entertainment system. Apart from Hailey's contribution to the canon, there have been 16 other films and TV shows called simply *Hotel*, and they come from everywhere — France, India, Japan. Strangely, the one theme that occurs more often than not in the non-Hailey versions is that of a man or woman waiting alone in a hotel for a love who isn't returning for whatever reason.

Perhaps the most notorious of the hotel books that also became a movie and a television series is Stephen King's classic *The Shining*. I first read King's chilling novel when I was a kid who already had a healthy love of hotels and a real familiarity with the Royal York, so the hotel setting and haunting King prose held me in a tight grip from first page to last. In the novel a writer/teacher and his wife and young son spend a long winter alone as caretakers in a fictional hotel called the Overlook in the Colorado Rockies. Awful things happened in the hotel in the past possibly because it was built on an old Native American burial site. Slowly, the writer, Jack Torrance, descends into madness, the same insanity that appears to have befallen other caretakers in years gone by. The question posed seems to be: Does evil live in the walls and the fabrics of the Overlook, or has Jack been driven crazy simply by being alone in a huge old hotel in the dead of winter for months on end?

In the late 1970s, Kubrick wanted to explore the horror genre. Slasher or splatter horror films were coming out weekly at the time and making small fortunes, which prompted Kubrick to think of making a movie that was as intellectually stimulating as it was scary. So he instructed his assistant to buy the ten top-selling horror novels of the day. She reported sitting outside his closed door, listening to book after book thump against a wall. Kubrick would read ten or 15 pages, then throw the book away. Eventually, 20 minutes went by without any thumping, then a half-hour, then an hour. The assistant peeked inside the office to see Kubrick engrossed in *The Shining*.

Kubrick was American but chose to live and work in Britain where he made all his movies no matter where they were set (he even shot a Vietnam War film, *Full Metal Jacket*, there). He created much of the Overlook on soundstages and backlots at Elstree Studios, but the exteriors of the hotel were shot by a second unit at Timberline Lodge on Mount Hood in Oregon. However, the managers of the Timberline would only grant permission to use their property in the film if Kubrick took out a reference to room 217 as the place where all the notorious and gruesome things happen. They were scared that no one would ever want to stay in that room again! Kubrick complied and changed the room number to 237, which isn't a number the Timberline uses. But what really made the hotel aspect of the film so effective was the use of long hallways, huge, ornate ballrooms, and sumptuous lobbies filled with comfortable furniture and giant fireplaces — the ambience of delightfully comfortable isolation.

As Torrance slips into madness, that isolation is one of the triggers, but as a hotel lover, I was intrigued by the scenes where Jack loses himself in delusions and believes he isn't alone but in a giant, noisy celebration in a ballroom filled with people. That's one of the interesting things about living in a hotel. You can be absolutely solitary in a socially relaxed crowd if you want. The choice is entirely yours. If you need to be blanketed in the comfort of your suite, you only need to shut the door and you're in your own little world. And if you feel the need to be around people, you're an elevator ride from that, as well.

The Shining, both novel and film, wonderfully captures the essence of what makes big, old hotels great: when you're there, you're exposed to the collective energies of all that took place before you. Venerable hotels wear their history like comfortable old sweaters. When The Shining became a 1997 television mini-series, the locations were a lot more authentic to the book than were Kubrick's. King wrote the teleplay for the TV series himself, while Kubrick created his own screenplay with Diane Johnson, his writing partner. The miniseries' director, Mick Garris, shot the show in Colorado, using the Stanley Hotel in Estes Park as his setting. This version, in which Stephen Webber plays Jack Torrance in a less manic, strangely more effective manner than Jack Nicholson does, stays much closer to the tone and substance of the novel.

But of all the hotel horror books that have been made into movies, one of the most wildly entertaining is 1408, which few people seem to have seen. Again the story was hatched in the darkly fertile mind of Stephen King. However, what is wonderfully odd about the narrative this time is that while it was actually inspired by a real guy and a real (supposedly) series of events, the tale itself was never intended as anything more than an example in King's instruction book On Writing of how to revise short stories. As he began penning the story for that purpose, King found himself getting deeper and deeper into it until it became a fully realized novella.

The story concerns a writer whose specialty is debunking paranormal myths. In the course of his research he is drawn to the dreaded room 1408 in the Dolphin Hotel in New York City, a suite that is said to be so haunted that the establishment has permanently declared the room off-limits. The writer, played by John Cusack, is convinced this will be his next great investigation, even though the manager of the hotel, played by Samuel L. Jackson, tells him that in the hotel's 95-year history 56 people have died in the room and that people never seem to last more than an hour once inside. Again King employs the notion that big, old hotels contain a lot of stored-up energy from all the different people who have come and gone and all the events that have transpired within their walls. For my money this film (and story) far out-creeps *The Shining* in terms of hotel horror. The inspiration for the tale was derived from the real-life activities of parapsychologist Christopher Chacon's investigation of the notoriously haunted suite of Hotel Del Coronado in Coronado, California.

Even directors such as Quentin Tarantino and Robert Rodriguez got into the old-hotel-as-perfect-setting realm when they collaborated with two other hot young directors, Alexandre Rockwell and Allison Anders, on the 1995 anthology film *Four Rooms*. (Actually, the movie was supposed to be called *Five Rooms*, since Richard Linklater was slated to do a segment, as well, but dropped out before production began.) This film is set on New Year's Eve at the venerable Mon Signor Hotel in Hollywood. It is the first night on the job for a new bellman played by Tim Roth (the role was written specifically for Steve Buscemi, who ultimately had to turn it down due to scheduling reasons) who has to deal with four crazy sets of guests during his inaugural shift. West Hollywood's Chateau Marmont was used during the shooting.

Of all the movies, television shows, and novels set in or about hotels, perhaps the grandest of them all is *Grand Hotel* from 1932. It stars Greta Garbo, who utters her signature line and somewhat prophetic statement, "I want to be alone," in the film. Based on a

Broadway show adapted from a German play about the life and times of a luxurious Berlin hotel, this movie was audacious for a number of reasons. First, it was one of the initial films to buck the two-star formula of the day. Studio bosses, especially young Irving Thalberg who was running Metro-Goldwyn-Mayer at the time, believed that for a movie to be cost-effective no more than two big stars could be in it, otherwise salaries would cause the film to be budget-heavy and the studio would be unable to recoup its expenses. *Grand Hotel* featured the top five stars in the MGM stable and ended up being one of the biggest-grossing movies in the history of the studio up to that point. The film is still the only picture to win the Best Picture Oscar without being nominated in any other category.

Garbo and co-star Joan Crawford (who never appear in any scenes together) also made *Grand Hotel* legendary for their monumentally ridiculous diva behaviour while working on the set. There were two things that Garbo really hated: lateness and Marlene Dietrich. So, because Joan Crawford was terribly angry that Garbo was getting top billing in *Grand Hotel*, she exacted a bit of revenge by always showing up late and playing Marlene Dietrich records loudly between the shooting of scenes. Garbo, for her part, demanded that the colossal and ornate hotel set be lit a smoky red during rehearsals to get her in a romantic mood.

Incidentally, the original MGM Grand Hotel in Las Vegas (now where Bally's is) was designed to resemble the Berlin hotel built on the MGM soundstages for *Grand Hotel*. As a further side note, Garbo herself lived in the Fairmont Miramar, a hotel in Santa Monica, California, in the 1920s and presumably found some of the solitude she sought.

≈ ≈ ≈

The Fairmont Miramar is known as a celebrity hideaway and has been such since Greta Garbo famously made it one. She was followed in the 1930s by Jean Harlow, who lived in the Miramar for years. In the 1950s, Marilyn Monroe, who spent most of her Hollywood days in hotels, resided in the Miramar. Most recently the Miramar was the hotel Britney Spears lived in while her Malibu mansion was being renovated.

Because of my long and deep history with Toronto's Royal York, I tend to use that hotel as the standard by which I compare all others. In Los Angeles, as I mentioned earlier, I have a great fondness for Chateau Marmont due to its colourful Hollywood history. However, the L.A. hotel I most closely associate with the Royal York is a lovely place on Stone Canyon Road called Hotel Bel-Air. The Bel-Air has been around since 1946 but was originally built as a relaxing, secluded office space to service the Bel-Air Estates development mushrooming in the canyon area in the early 1950s. The structures that now make up the Bel-Air were bought by Joseph Drown, a Texan, who converted it into a 91-room hotel. He added lush grounds, a wonderful swan lake (with swans so big they look almost prehistoric), and a footbridge that guests must cross to enter the hotel.

Part of the charm of the Bel-Air is its relative seclusion deep in a canyon surrounded by trees and vegetation. When I stayed there, despite the relative isolation, I could still jog from the hotel to Sunset Boulevard in 20 minutes, only to get lost on a daily basis on the way back in the seemingly endless, twisty canyon roads. I spent a fair amount of time at the Bel-Air a few years ago and fell in love instantly with the place when I was told I'd be staying in the same suite Marilyn Monroe once occupied. As I was being shown to my suite by the delightful (and award-winning) concierge Charles Fitzer, we passed the large palm-tree-ringed oval swimming pool. Charles pointed out the area and the chair that John Wayne used when he lived at the Bel-Air. My suite was sumptuous and comfortable, with a working wood fireplace and a private patio.

The hotel is spread out over a number of acres, so no suite is higher than the second floor. You are either on the ground or one up. As with many older, classy hotels that attract movie people, an air of eccentricity and surrealism is part of the day and night there. It's as if you're always waiting for something strange to happen, and usually you don't have long to wait. While I was there a typical Southern California heat wave scorched the landscape. In the canyon where the Bel-Air is situated it was marginally cooler, but the sun still seared skin as if it were in a blast furnace. Nevertheless, I was determined to do my usual morning laps in the big pool no matter what.

That first morning I did my laps alone, since it was pretty early. The only other creature nearby was a strange, colourful,

At Hotel Bel-Air in Los Angeles you can meet anyone from former U.S. First Lady Nancy Reagan to actor Daniel Day-Lewis.

duck-like bird that splashed around with me here and there. After swimming I sat in one of the lounge chairs with a book and the *Los Angeles Times* to dry off. Without seeing them until the last second, I was flanked by two guys in black suits. I assumed at first that they were with the hotel, but they seemed a bit too officious for that upon closer inspection. Then one spoke to me. "Good morning, sir. We were just wondering if you wouldn't find it even more comfortable over in that area there." He indicated the other end of the pool.

I chuckled and asked the fellow why he was making such a suggestion. He produced credentials that identified him as an agent of the U.S. Secret Service and explained that someone under the Secret Service's protection took morning tea where I was sitting. They would appreciate it awfully if I'd change spots for a while.

Seeing no point in arguing with two Secret Service agents, especially over a poolside chair, I moved to the spot they indicated and even asked them if my choice was okay. They waved and said it was. A tea service with fine china and silver was set up, and the two guys returned with former First Lady Nancy Reagan and a lady guest. Mrs. Reagan waved in my direction and mouthed the words "Thank you." I thought that was nice, though I was sure that moving locations wasn't actually a decision I could really make.

A few mornings later I was back in the pool doing my laps. There were a few people around the pool reading the morning paper and drinking coffee, but I was swimming alone. I noticed someone come in and take notice of the book I was reading. It was lying on my lounge chair. (I was reading a new book that re-examined the famous mutiny on the *Bounty*, with an eye toward realism over seafaring drama.) The fellow then stepped to the pool and hunched down to say something to me as I swam close. "Would you mind if I took a look at your book? I'll mind not to lose your page." I told him he was welcome to it. The guy was actor Daniel Day-Lewis, after all.

When I finished swimming, I got out of the pool and sat next to where Day-Lewis reclined. He told me he had a particular interest in the *Bounty* story, since he had done something on it himself years ago. I said I was well aware of that. Day-Lewis had played Master's Mate John Fryer in the Anthony Hopkins/Mel Gibson film *The Bounty*.

"Ah, you know it?" he asked.

I told him I was an admirer of the movie and that it would have been fantastic if it had been made as originally planned as a giant two-part epic directed by David Lean (New Zealander Roger Donaldson ending up doing it instead). I said it would have been a spellbinding bit of cinema to have Lean reunited with his *Lawrence of Arabia* screenwriter Robert Bolt for such a saga. Part one would have been the voyage and the mutiny, while part two would have been the unbelievable feat of seamanship performed by the cut-adrift Captain William Bligh, who piloted a launch for months with no food or water and got his men to safety.

Day-Lewis studied me with a strange smile. "My, my, you know an awful lot about that film. May I ask why you know all that?"

I explained what I did, and we conversed for more than an hour, but not about films or acting. Instead we chatted about the mutiny on the *Bounty* and what life at sea must have been like. When he left for his meeting, we shook hands and exchanged pleasantries. I never saw Daniel Day-Lewis again in person, but my admiration for him as an actor doubled because of that accidental meeting at the Bel-Air. His intelligence and esoteric wonder about what other people think and feel are the reasons he's a great actor.

One morning after a lovely breakfast with Charles Fitzer at an outdoor table, he asked if I'd like to see one of the bigger suites the hotel had to offer. He told me he could show me around the suite Oprah Winfrey kept on hold for her trips to California. I knew a woman who was a rabid Oprah fan, so I agreed to check it out. We strolled over, and once we got into the suite, it was pretty much what I expected it to be — spacious and comfortable. The suite came with its own private swimming pool, small fountain, and terrace. I thanked Charles for guiding me around the rooms, and as we were leaving, I grabbed a Bel-Air pen from one of the coffee tables and stuck it in my pocket. I wanted to give it to my Oprah-loving friend. When I eventually gave her the pen, she reacted as though I'd brought her a religious relic I'd snatched from the Vatican!

On the subject of older grand hotels, one of the oldest and grandest in the world has to be Château Frontenac in Quebec City. Château Frontenac belongs to the Fairmont family of hotels in Canada, many of which were originally built by Canadian Pacific Railway. When you see Château Frontenac looming above historic Quebec City, it almost seems as if the solid edifice has always been there and that the rest of the provincial capital grew up around it. There is such an awesome majesty about even the look of the place, let alone its interior, which is every bit as majestic and awesome. The hotel was actually designed by American architect Bruce Price and opened in 1893. It was named after Louis de Buade, Count of Frontenac, who was the governor of New France from 1672 to 1682 and from 1689 to 1698 and was responsible for building the nearby Citadelle.

Of the many times I've stayed at Château Frontenac, two stand out above all the rest. Coincidentally, I was in the same suite both times — a terrific one high up near the top of the hotel. The bedroom area had a low-sloped ceiling because of the configuration of the roof, and a hallway led to an enormous bathroom with an immense tub. Directly across from the tub was an alcove where a desk sat before a window that offered a stunning view of Quebec City. During that time, I was writing a magazine piece about Château Frontenac, which *The Guinness Book of Records* lists as holding the record for the most photographed hotel in the world.

Because of the assignment I was doing, I was treated to an extraordinary evening. I was asked to join a few members of the hotel management and public relations staff for dinner in a room that wasn't a designated dining area but an ornate sitting room. It was explained to me that the room was used at the 1943 Quebec Conference by President Franklin D. Roosevelt and Prime Minister Winston Churchill for relaxed conversations about the direction of the Second World War. The actual strategy meetings were held at the Citadelle, but when the two leaders talked off the record it was in the room where we were eating.

Dinner was a magnificent treat of French-Canadian cuisine, including a tourtière, a meat pie made from local game and the best I've ever had and no doubt ever will. As dinner wound down, a guest joined us. The door opened, and Louis de Buade, Count of Frontenac, strolled in. Of course, it was an actor playing the count, but his costume and wig were perfect. I thought this was a wonderful touch to the evening and rose to be introduced to him. I stuck out my hand to shake hands, but the count quickly pulled a pair of white gloves from his waistcoat and swatted my hands with them hard.

Momentarily, I was taken aback, then the count explained that since I was a commoner, it was highly inappropriate for me to approach him with such misguided familiarity, let alone

Château Frontenac in Quebec City is one of the Fairmont chain's grand old railway hotels. In the foreground is Auberge Saint-Antoine.

(Courtesy Fairmont Hotels & Resorts)

expect to touch him. I apologized. Then he told me that simply bowing before him was sufficient. I frowned and leaned toward a public relations woman beside me. "Is he actually expecting me to bow to him?"

She winked and whispered, "Just play along."

So I made a big gesture of bowing with sweeping arms before the count. He nodded and strode regally over to his chair at the end of the table; I was seated to his left. Of course, he stood behind his chair, indicating I was to pull it out for him. I played along. The count began a history lesson that was so engrossing and detailed that within 15 minutes I completely lost touch with reality and started thinking he actually was the Count of Frontenac. I even asked him questions and talked to him as if he were the real McCoy. "When you arrived here, Count, those first years must have been awfully challenging, given how inhospitable nature can be in this region." He answered with such depth, with such authority of feeling, that I was truly mesmerized. After about 90 minutes, he got up to leave. Without prompting, I bowed to him very naturally, then he whipped out his sword and placed it on my shoulder. I almost cried. It was an incredible evening, and a brilliant public relations tool.

Another memorable time at Château Frontenac was when I interviewed the actors in a film — the thriller *Taking Lives* starring Angelina Jolie and Ethan Hawke — that was shooting there and around Quebec City and Montreal. One day I was sitting on the set when the production took over the entrance-way to the hotel for a couple of shots of Angelina's character first arriving in a car, then rushing out the door for another scene to be used later in the film. It was a windy day, so there was a lot of waiting around for clouds to clear in order to match the various angles of the shots in terms of lighting. After I got the official interview stuff completed with Jolie and casually

related some of the hotel's history, I recounted my meeting
with the Count of Frontenac himself. Then I told the actress
that in 1953 Alfred Hitchcock was so impressed by Château
Frontenac that he used it for the thriller *I Confess*.

This piqued her interest. "Was that the one where
Montgomery Clift played the Catholic priest?" she asked.

I told her that was indeed the picture. Karl Malden, who co-
starred in the film, had told me great stories about how much he
loved shooting in Quebec City. At the time it was so remote and
unused as a film location that it had an exotic freshness about it.
Jolie called over an assistant and asked her to run out and find
her a DVD of *I Confess*. She then told me that if we saw each
other on the set again we could discuss the Hitchcock movie. I
thought that was a great idea but never did get the opportunity.

There is another hotel in Quebec City that also has a
great history, even though it is relatively new, only a few years
old, in fact. Because of where it is and what was discovered
when construction began, the hotel took on a whole new
atmosphere and design. It's called Auberge Saint-Antoine.
My friend and ace travel public relations person Ann Layton
of Siren Communications introduced me to this hotel. She
arranged for me to spend some time in the place and meet
Llewellyn Price, its owner.

The story of this multi-faceted hotel is quite interesting.
It began when the Price family (of the Abitibi-Price pulp and
paper empire) bought a collection of rundown, abandoned
warehouses, an apartment house, and a parking lot on prime
property facing the St. Lawrence River. In 1992 they converted part of the collection of buildings into a small inn called
Auberge Saint-Antoine. It had only 23 comfortable rooms
then. In 1995 the second phase of the hotel, Maison Hunt,
opened. It was the old apartment house restored to reflect

its 18th-century heritage. Now the *auberge* had eight more suites, but these new ones were each completely unique and had a specific historical theme reflected in their decor. A third phase was planned that involved digging up the parking lot and erecting an ultra-slick, hip boutique hotel, but because of the location's historical significance, the Quebec government stepped in.

"It was suggested to us that we do a bit of an archaeological dig, a survey, beforehand to determine if there wasn't something of historical value there," Price told me. "Of course, we could only benefit by that, too, so we entered into a partnership with the city, the Ministry of Culture and Communications of Quebec, and the Council of Monuments and Historical Sites of Quebec, and brought in experts from Laval University to begin the dig."

That dig turned up a virtual treasure trove of museum-quality pieces large and small and revealed a 17th-century cannon battery complete with intact walls and cannons as well as a wealth of dishes, pottery, utensils, and weapons. "We decided to build the 63-room modern boutique hotel on the site," Price said, "but make everything that was discovered part of the hotel. The walls and cannons are perfectly preserved as part of the lobby, and the artifacts we found are displayed in the hallways under glass, so the hotel is a modern hotel and a museum of the history of the very site it was built on, going back 300 or more years."

While Auberge Saint-Antoine is a lovely hotel, and I enjoyed every minute of my several visits there, the museum-like aspect is sometimes a bit distracting. In the comfortable suites, artifacts are displayed under glass on end tables, in the coffee tables, the desk, and the walls outside doors. It gives the place a reverential sort of vibe, so much so that you don't dare put a soft drink can anywhere. Still, the boldness of creating a slick, ultra-modern hotel with a historical theme running through every corner is admirable.

Quebec City's Auberge Saint-Antoine weds history to modern convenience to create a unique boutique hotel.

Perhaps one of the most endearing and lovable characters from film and literature who brings together hotel living and the beauty of old-world hotels is Eloise, the perennial six-year-old girl who lives in the Plaza Hotel in New York City. The Plaza (now owned by Fairmont) is to New York City what the Royal York is to Toronto — a beacon, a place of history, grace, and class that's larger than its already immense iconic reputation. The first time I had the opportunity to visit New York I wanted to go to the Plaza and stroll through its grand lobby. When I did so, one of the first things I saw was the portrait of Eloise painted by illustrator Hilary Knight. My notions of the Plaza were formed by Eloise and by Neil Simon's play and film *Plaza Suite*, and here I was standing in, as Archie Bunker once said, "the middle of their midst."

This history of the Plaza and the Royal York has a lot of similarities, which probably explains why the hotels have, in some respects, similar appearances and characteristics. The Plaza is located in a prime Manhattan location: Fifth Avenue and Central Park South. It was designed by the American architect Henry Janey Hardenbergh to be "the greatest hotel in the world." The Plaza opened on October 1, 1907, and was built on the site of another hotel called the Plaza, which was knocked down to be replaced by the current, grander building. No expense was spared to erect this 19-storey French Renaissance château-like structure complete with marble lobbies, solid mahogany doors, 1,650 crystal chandeliers, Swiss organdy curtains, linens manufactured privately for the exclusive use of guests, and gold-encrusted china.

In the books by New York show business figure Kay Thompson, Eloise lives in a suite on the "tippy-top floor" of the Plaza. Tall and slender with a deep, breathy voice, Thompson first invented her make-believe character in 1948 when she arrived late for a nightclub performance. The nightclub owner reputedly shouted at her, "Who do you think you are?"

Thompson answered in a little girl voice, "I am Eloise!" and proceeded to lay the blame for her tardiness on her little girl alter ego. Over the next few years, the singer/dancer incorporated the precocious Eloise into her stage act. In 1954 Thompson's friends encouraged her to put Eloise on paper in a children's book. Thompson was introduced to illustrator Hilary Knight, whom it was thought could bring Eloise to life. Over Christmas of that year, Knight sent Thompson a Christmas card with her first impression of what Eloise would look like riding in a sleigh with Santa Claus. Thompson glanced at the picture and said, "It was immediate recognition on my part. There she was. In person."

Knight moved into the Plaza with Thompson, who had been living there for years, to work on the first book. While the collaborators engaged in "writing, editing, laughing, outlining, cutting, pasting, laughing again, reading out loud, laughing some more," it seemed natural to have Eloise live in the Plaza. The idea flowered fully for Thompson when she thought of Liza Minnelli, her own goddaughter, who was often left in the company and care of hotel staffers while mother Judy Garland was on the set of a film or singing in a club or recording an album. Now everything fitted together like a Swiss watch. Eloise would show up at weddings she wasn't invited to, and she would crash meetings and parties and interrupt all sorts of different people in the hotel. The inaugural book, Eloise, was published on November 28, 1955, and was so successful that offers to write more installments were immediate, as were requests to record versions of the stories, do product endorsements, and authorize dramatizations of Eloise's life. Thompson and Knight then set up Eloise Ltd., with the Plaza, of course, as their headquarters.

In 1956 Thompson allowed the TV anthology series *Playhouse 90* to do a show adapted from her book. It was billed as "Eloise — based on the hilarious bestselling story about the sprightly six-year-old girl who runs — and often runs ragged — the lives of the celebrated guests and devoted employees of a distinguished New York hotel." But the writer who penned the teleplay strayed wildly from the basic innocence and good nature of the character and created a drama involving Eloise being caught in the middle of her parents' divorce and the hotel being filled with intrigue and scoundrels. The reviews of the show were terrible, and people who loved the books completely rejected this dramatization. Thompson was so angry about what had been done to her book that she vowed never again to allow her character to be dramatized in another medium.

Later in the 1950s three more Eloise books were published, and Thompson became a celebrity mainstay at the Plaza where she organized huge tea parties for fans and entertained them

(Courtesy Fairmont Hotels & Resorts)

New York City's fabled Plaza Hotel is best known as the home of the delightful but fictional Eloise.

with Eloise stories. In 1958 she helped create the children's menu at the Plaza that features such dishes as "Teeny Weenies" and "Eggs Eloise." For a number of years there was a special room at the Plaza named the Eloise Room. It was a large sitting room where guests could relax and mingle. There was also, for a while, an ice-cream parlour in the Plaza called the Eloise.

By 1989 the Eloise books had been in constant print for decades and were huge bestsellers. At the Plaza a new owner, Donald Trump, wanted to use the image of Eloise in an advertising campaign for the hotel. Hilary Knight was brought in to design special children's suites in the hotel that featured murals on the walls commemorating the adventures of Eloise. She was also asked to design children's menus with Eloise drawings on them. But Thompson didn't like Trump and refused to allow him to exploit her character to sell his hotel. The entertainer's aversion to Trump had arisen after the financier took control of the Plaza. Thompson had been living in the hotel for many years free of charge because the previous owners were eternally grateful to her for putting their hotel on the map in such a unique and indelible way. Trump, however, insisted that Thompson pay for her suite. Thompson said if that was the case then Trump would have to start paying her for the rights to use her character.

Eloise, by that time, had become world-famous and had made the Plaza renowned along with her. Knight painted a portrait of Eloise that hung in the Palm Court (the place where Eloise goes for lunch when it's raining). That picture became a sort of Mona Lisa for the Plaza. Mothers and daughters came to the Palm Court for tea just to look at it. Then one night during a raucous college frat-boy party the portrait was stolen and never recovered. Knight was brought in to do another painting to replace the missing one when, it is said, Princess Grace of Monaco arrived with her children to see the portrait and was vocally dismayed that she had come all that way to look at an empty wall. The new painting of Eloise, the one I first saw, now hangs on the wall opposite the Palm Court.

While Eloise's parents are never part of the action of the books, the child does have a nanny and a couple of companions, specifically her pug dog, Weenie, and her turtle, Skipperdee. However, it wasn't until after Thompson died in 1998 in her early nineties that readers were able to see Eloise come to life again on the screen. The rights to the character and the books passed to Thompson's sister, Blanche Hurd, who gave consent for a number of TV movies and straight-to-DVD feature-film versions using the Eloise character. In 2003 two TV movies were made based on the character that featured none other than Julie Andrews as Nanny. Three years later an animated series debuted and is a solid seller on DVD. It boasts the voice of Lynn Redgrave as Nanny. At this writing there is a big-screen picture being planned around Eloise that will star Uma Thurman as Nanny. To this day, one of the bestselling items in the Plaza's gift shop is the postcard version of the Knight portrait of Eloise.

So when people hear my story of living in the Royal York and say, "You're just like the little girl Eloise," I not only take that as a supreme compliment but have to admit that, yes, I am Eloise!

For a number of years I covered the Toronto International Film Festival for *Reel to Real*, a television show I co-produced and co-hosted in the InterContinental Hotel on Bloor Street West. We secured a suite, turned it into a mini-studio where we interviewed actors and filmmakers, and shot segments for the shows during the festival. I literally moved into the suite for a few weeks amid the camera equipment, lighting gear, and all the other equipment necessary to make a daily television show on location. Year after year I lived for those weeks in the space left over in the suite as people such as Ed Harris, Kathryn Bigelow, Eric Bana, Joaquin Phoenix, Monica Bellucci, and many others filed in and out for interviews and various eccentric adventures. Every day I ate at least once or twice in the main all-day restaurant and came to know the menu as if I'd designed it myself.

During those years, I got quite familiar with InterContinental's hotels as a brand. Later I visited other hotels in the chain in Montreal and in Cannes, France, but I truly appreciated brand familiarity as supremely important when I was asked to do a magazine story in Seoul, South Korea. The scenario was quite surreal. I was called on the phone by the editor of *Dolce Vita*, a magazine I'd been contributing to for a few years. The editor asked if I had plans the following week. I told her no, and she asked if I wanted to go to Seoul. Although I'd never been to Asia at that point in my life and Seoul wasn't somewhere I'd given much thought about visiting, I agreed to go. I flew to Los Angeles (five hours from Toronto), then lay over for a couple of hours before boarding a Korean Air jet for Seoul's Incheon International Airport (13 hours more on a plane). When I arrived in South Korea's capital, I was met by a smiling guide/driver who enthusiastically welcomed me, asked how my flight was, and told me I'd be relaxing in my suite at the COEX InterContinental inside an hour.

Seoul is a massive city, and the COEX InterContinental is a huge hotel in the centre of it. When I arrived in the lobby of the COEX, I was surprised that it resembled a combination of the lobbies of the two InterContinental hotels in Toronto (the other InterContinental is on Front Street West). After I got to my suite 22 storeys up, I was immediately struck by the fact that it looked similar to the suite we used to shoot the interviews at the InterContinental in Toronto. So while I was still a bit freaked out about being in this giant Asian city, I was very much at ease because I knew what to anticipate inside the hotel. Outside, in Seoul, I had no idea what to expect, but inside my suite I was relaxed and comfortable and knew where everything was and was familiar with everything, including the scent of the shampoo in the bathroom. The one big difference was that the COEX InterContinental was considerably more technologically advanced than I was used to, including air conditioning and lights that seemed able to sense when I was in the room, switching on and off accordingly.

During my time in Seoul, I crawled around in a tunnel in the Demilitarized Zone between North and South Korea and glanced across the fence into the former at a soldier staring back at me. I made a Korean paper lantern with a group of schoolchildren, toured a palace, lay on a bed that a Korean princess was murdered on, and had lunch in a high-tech restaurant with a glass floor that was about 60 floors above the bustling city between two colossal office towers. But none of those experiences compared to the surreal episodes I had each day at the health club and then at the restaurant, The Brasserie, in the hotel, where I ate breakfast each morning.

To this day, living as I do in the Royal York, I put in an hour's worth of laps in the swimming pool before breakfast, then commence working. My time in Seoul was no different. I timed it so I could swim for an hour and have breakfast in The Brasserie before meeting my guide for whatever was planned for that day.

The health club at the COEX (called the Cosmopolitan Fitness Club) is state-of-the-art. That first morning when I headed down for a swim I was given a rubber bathing cap by a pretty young Korean female pool attendant. I handed it back because I don't wear bathing caps. She smiled and returned it to me. I passed it back and told her I didn't use bathing caps. She then said in broken but serviceable English that wearing a bathing cap was a requirement for swimming in the pool. I apologized and said I would wear the cap if that was the rule.

When I got into the pool, I tried to put the cap on, but it kept sliding up my skull and off. The young Korean woman noticed I was having trouble and entered the pool area to help. She offered to put it on for me, but given my height (six foot four) and hers (not a hair over five feet), I literally had to get on my knees in front of her as she expertly snapped the cap on my head, where it stayed in place for the whole hour. Every subsequent morning I went down for the swim, and she put the cap on for me.

After swimming I went to The Brasserie for breakfast because I wanted to have one meal of the day that was familiar to me, since everything else I would eat during the day would be authentic Korean. The Brasserie looked almost exactly the same as the all-day restaurant at the InterContinental on Bloor Street in Toronto, only much bigger to reflect the size of the hotel. At The Brasserie I could have a bowl of oatmeal and some scrambled eggs and toast and coffee. On my first morning there I made the mistake of allowing the waiter to put kimchi in front of me. He explained that Koreans usually ate kimchi at every meal and that while there were many varieties of kimchi (there is actually a Kimchi Field Museum in Seoul), the kind I was exposed to was made from fermented cabbage stuffed with veg-etables and seasonings (perhaps even nitroglycerin!).

I made the mistake that first morning of having oatmeal, then getting some eggs and toast and letting the waiter lay some kimchi on me. It was so spicy and tasted so diabolically vile that once I swallowed it I thought it might actually kill me. I drank about seven glasses of water and had three cups of coffee, but still the raging esophageal wildfire remained and a taste that couldn't be described in words still lingered. At virtually every other meal I had in Korea, including every breakfast at The Brasserie, I was offered kimchi. Finally, I told my regular Brasserie waiter that if he dared bring kimchi to the table again, I would have no choice but to throw it on the floor. He never brought me more and seemed to go out of his way to not even mention it. Once, he even covered the word *kimchi* on a special addition to the menu so I wouldn't have to think about it. That was nice of him and much appreciated.

Looking back on my time in Seoul, I have nothing but fondness, kimchi notwithstanding, and I do believe that a large part of that was because of the comfortable and familiar elements of the hotel I was living in. I felt safe and at ease in a foreign land I'd never been to before because when I was in my suite at night and when I woke up in the morning, there was no culture shock, just comfort that a familiar brand provided.

Las Vegas hotels belong in a category by themselves. In fact, even to call a lot of them hotels is to do them a great injustice. They are more like teeming glitter domes the size of small cities. I've spent time in a number of Las Vegas hotels, and the truly amazing thing is that they are all pretty much the same in that they all come complete with about 20 first-class restaurants apiece, world-class shopping, and usually a state-of-the-art theatre or two. And, of course, the one significant thing they all share is gambling. But what makes these gargantuan monuments to excess unique is that while they are all the same, they are all also utterly and completely different.

The trend of people living in hotels is probably more prevalent in Las Vegas than anywhere else on earth. Most long-time residents are performers of one stripe or another. Often when headliners are brought to Las Vegas to do shows in house theatres, a luxurious suite comes with the deal. Some Las Vegas headliners sign contracts that run for several years. Barry Manilow's suite at the Mirage during his stint there was so grand and luxurious that it had its own waterfall. When French-Canadian songbird Céline Dion signed for a five-year run at Caesars Palace, the deal included a $60 million theatre built for her stage show.

One of the most interesting permanent hotel residents in Las Vegas is magician and illusionist Criss Angel, who lives in a large penthouse suite in the pyramid-shaped Luxor Hotel, which emits a laser beam straight up from its apex that is so powerful it can be seen from the moon. Angel performs at the Luxor, and a good deal of his television show, *Mindfreak*, is shot there, as well.

I first met the entertainer completely by accident at a time when I didn't know who he was. I was in Las Vegas doing a magazine piece about a new hotel, the Palazzo, at the other end of the strip from the Luxor. When my stint there was done, the assistant manager of the hotel arranged for a lovely bronze-coloured stretch limo to take me to the airport. As I was climbing into the car, the assistant manager asked if I'd mind if someone rode along with me to the airport. My companion was described as a high-profile star who was on his way to the airport to meet a lady friend flying in from Los Angeles on a private jet. He wanted to meet her without drawing attention.

Of course, I was intrigued, and since it was their limo, I said I'd be happy to share the ride. A few minutes later a dude who looked like a rock star climbed into the back of the limo.

Wearing ripped jeans, a scruffy T-shirt that probably cost $200, a thin leather jacket, and lots of chains and silver rings, he greeted me with a smile and an outstretched hand. "Thanks, man, I really appreciate you letting me share your ride."

I told him it was my pleasure and that it would be nice to have company. For the first half of the trip we talked about the various hotels we'd been to in Las Vegas. He then told me he lived in the Luxor but phrased the statement as if he were telling me something I already knew.

At this point I still didn't have any idea who this character was. I thought he was a member of a heavy metal band named after some infectious disease or other. When we arrived at the airport via a back way that led to a couple of private jet hangars, he extended a hand again. "Hey, thanks, man. Thanks for being cool about this. Most people ask me to perform for them. It was nice to just sit and talk."

I smiled but didn't have a clue what he was talking about. *Ask him to perform?* Was he saying that people expected him to break into death metal tunes in the backs of cars?

As he got out, he asked, "Do you have a dollar bill?" I did and fished it out of my pocket and gave it to him. When he reached for the bill and took it between his thumb and forefinger before I could let it go, he said, "I only asked you for a buck, bro."

I glanced down. I was holding a $100 bill! I was amazed and more than a little freaked out. (I'd been in Las Vegas for a week and had nothing close to a $100 bill in my pocket.)

Angel grinned once more and slapped me on the shoulder. "Next time you're in town drop by the Luxor. We'll have a drink or six and talk about hotel life."

I told him I'd do that, even though I still didn't know who he was. As Angel disappeared into the hangar, I glanced at the $100 bill in my hand. The driver looked back at me and chuckled.

"Who the fuck was that guy?" I asked.

The driver shook his head and asked me if I was kidding him.

"I was holding a single. I never let go of it, not even for an instant. That dude touched it, and it turned into a hundred."

The driver laughed. "Yeah, man, that cat's scary — like he has some kind of weird connection with the other side."

I was dumbfounded again and thought: *The other side of what?*

Jump ahead six months or so. By this time I knew who Criss Angel was, I had watched (and loved) his TV show *Mindfreak*, I had read his autobiography, and I was back in Las Vegas for another magazine story and was gathering material for *The Suite Life*. So I was now definitely interested in looking up Angel, as he'd suggested, to talk to him about living in the Luxor, which by then he'd been doing for just over three years.

By this time Angel was a bona fide Las Vegas superstar. Here the distinction must be drawn between Las Vegas superstars and ordinary ones. It isn't uncommon for performers in Las Vegas to earn six figures weekly, have their images plastered on billboards bigger than movie screens, and fill auditoriums on a daily basis with fans paying a couple of hundred dollars a ticket, while at the same time have virtually no one know who they are 20 minutes outside the Vegas city limits,. How many people have heard of a strange red-headed comedian named Carrot Top? In Las Vegas that guy is a major draw and a huge star.

Criss Angel doesn't fall into that category. Because of his TV show and his autobiography, he is well-known and wildly successful. Of course, his work in Las Vegas and his new show combining his act with Cirque du Soleil (called *Believe*) put Angel into the quarter-million-dollar-per-week-plus stratosphere. An entire shop in the Luxor sells nothing but Criss

Angel logo wear and posters and other assorted Angel merchandise. The parking garage at the Luxor has a special area where Angel's black Lamborghini, black Rolls-Royce, and various custom-made choppers reside. Angel's suite in the Luxor is really big, but most high-roller suites are. He has windows that give him panoramic views in every direction, huge, comfortable couches and chairs, a massive bed, and lots and lots of space.

When we started talking about living in a hotel, he said, "The thing that's interesting is how I've come to befriend and greatly appreciate a lot of the hotel staff and the silent, invisible workers most people don't even notice. The people who work the kitchen, the guys at the door, the security guys, they're the people who keep things running in this place. I live in comfort because of those people, not the executives."

I asked Angel if there was anything he didn't like about living in a hotel, anything he found bothersome or inconvenient. "Oh, man, I've got it very good here, man, very good. If there's anything negative about the experience, it would be too minor even to mention." I pressed him, citing my own curiosity and desire to compare notes as a fellow hotel resident. "Okay, if I had to come up with one thing about living here permanently, it would have to be that this place is so fucking big! To get from here to over there requires a fucking excursion. But when weighed against the comforts and luxuries laid on me here, the added time to get around is a small price to pay."

Then I asked Angel, as an illusionist, if he noticed the swirling collective energies of all the people past and present who have shared his space in the hotel. "Are you kidding me? I feed off those energies, man. Hotels are full of that kind of lingering energy, especially here in Las Vegas. A kind of high-octane, adrenaline-fuelled energy is all around you here. You feel it crackling around you as soon as you walk in. This is a place where anything you can possibly imagine can happen and often the experience will include something you'd not even dare to imagine. People do things in hotels they normally would just imagine doing but never would think of actually doing. Then the collective energies they come into contact with here give them the freedom and the spirit to live what they dreamed or imagined."

The hotels on the Las Vegas strip aren't so much cities within cities as giant indoor theme parks. One of the most interesting hotel experiences I've ever had in Las Vegas was that first trip when I met Criss Angel after staying in the Palazzo. The hotel, which was new, wanted to get more attention, so I was there for a week or so writing a story about the place for *Dolce Vita* magazine. The Palazzo was built as a kind of sister hotel to the dazzling Venetian Hotel next door. The motivation behind the creation of the Palazzo was the fact that Steve Wynn, owner of Wynn's and a bunch of other properties in Las Vegas, opened Encore, a companion tower to his main hotel. Since Las Vegas

Everything in Las Vegas is larger than life, including hotels such as the Palazzo.

is essentially run by a handful of guys playing a high-stakes game of "mine's bigger than yours," that meant if Wynn opened a second hotel tower, the owners of the Venetian would have to erect an even larger mate for its first establishment.

Truly, the Palazzo is gargantuan. The moment you stroll into its lobby — a huge reception area with marble columns and giant fountains — you really do feel as if you've entered a palace. After checking in, you're given a map to locate the right elevator so you can set about finding your suite. My suite in the Palazzo was considered pretty standard in Vegas, which meant it was colossal. I had two mammoth beds, a huge bathroom with a television, and a generous sunken living room with an L-shaped sofa that extended halfway around the living room. The suite also contained an oversized desk and an immense flat-screen TV. A vast picture window gave me a breathtaking view of the mountains and sunrises, while the drapes were hydraulically controlled by remote control.

The hotel had only been open for about seven months when I moved in to write the story, yet the furniture already seemed well used. Tables were scratched and scuffed, and the couch had small tears and holes in its fabric. This was a clear indication of the wear and tear that hard-living guests inflict upon Vegas strip hotels. Such intense activity ages a hotel ten times faster than the normal course of affairs for a hotel anywhere else in the world. While most premier hotels have a main restaurant and a few smaller eateries designed for quick breakfasts and lunches, Vegas strip hotels feel the need for at least 15 world-class restaurants apiece.

One of the nicest eateries in the Palazzo is Carne Vino, a steak-and-wine establishment whose atmosphere is reminiscent of 1940s Broadway. Here the gaudy glitz of the strip is left behind to be replaced by the warmth of dark wood walls and tables. I had the best steak dinner I've ever had there and was treated to some lovely Hine Triomphe cognac to relax with afterward. In keeping with the old-school Manhattan vibe, there is a small men's barbershop boasting hot towels, straight-razor shaves, and the attention of Canadian Perry Gastis, a master barber. I went in to get my hair cut by Mr. Gastis, and not only was the experience fantastic but I became so relaxed in his chair that I felt as if I'd had a massage along with the shave and trim.

The focus of these enormous Vegas strip hotels is, of course, gambling. You can't reach the elevators without striding through the airplane-hangar-sized casino, and you can't arrive at the restaurants without negotiating a route that takes you through gaming tables or acres of slot machines. Since I'm not a fiend for that kind of action, I was free to explore the Palazzo without worrying how I was going to win back the money I'd just lost.

The old New York theme is everywhere in the Palazzo. The house show in the state-of-the-art theatre is *Jersey Boys*. The Shoppes, a shopping concourse, features an 85,000-square-foot Barney's New York, as well as a store that blew my mind when I first encountered it. Bauman's Rare Books seems truly out of place on the strip. Amid slot machines, glitz, and flash is one of the world's pre-eminent rare book dealers! I was fascinated as I quizzed the person on duty at Bauman's about the stock. I was told there were signed first editions of the novels of Ernest Hemingway and Ian Fleming, authentic letters written by Abraham Lincoln, and a signed first edition of James M. Cain's steamy crime novel *The Postman Always Rings Twice*. I was particularly interested in the last item until I saw the wallet-busting price tag. Every Friday at 4:00 p.m. you can drop by Bauman's for a tutorial on how to buy rare books.

There is also a Lamborghini dealership in the Palazzo that doubles as a restaurant and showroom that can be booked for parties among the exotic machines. One day I stopped by to check it out, and Ben Nef, a cool, laid-back, delightfully friendly sales representative, offered to take me out for a spin in a brand-new Lamborghini Gallardo. Of course, I jumped at the chance, having never driven around in a machine like that before. We blasted around the outskirts of Las Vegas on the highway leading to the desert and Red Rock. The experience was like roaring around in a fighter plane. When we returned to the Palazzo and the showroom, I was pumped by the ride. Nef then told me a true Vegas story. A guest from the United Arab Emirates came down for a quick test drive of a Lamborghini Gallardo and liked it so much that he gave Nef a business card and instructed him to send five to the address on the card (in assorted colours, naturally).

Before I left the Palazzo, I asked one of its managers if I could take a peek at a high-roller suite, or as I refer to it, a Big Loser Suite. Every large casino hotel has a few enormous suites that are never available for an average (or even VIP) guest to book. They are reserved for gamblers who have lost enough money to buy a small percentage of the hotel. The hotel comps gamblers these suites and attends to all their needs. Of course, the real purpose of this is obvious and insidious: by keeping the gambler in the hotel in a luxurious complimentary suite, it's very likely he or she has already lost a fortune to the casino and will return to try to win everything back and then lose even more.

I was taken to one of these palatial suites complete with its own massage table and sauna, a bedroom with a bed so huge it would fill most average hotel rooms wall to wall, and a staggering panoramic view of the strip and the surrounding mountains and desert. While the manager didn't divulge any names, and I didn't even ask for them, he did tell me that one guy stayed in this suite after losing the most money ever dropped at the casino — over

$8 million in a single two-day period. He relaxed in the high-roller suite, then dropped another $2 million trying to win back his $8 million before flying back to England.

One of my favourite and most eccentric conversations with a fellow hotel dweller was with legendary Irish rake and brilliant actor Richard Harris. He was in Toronto for the Toronto International Film Festival to support *My Kingdom*, a new film he was in. At that time he'd shot a couple of the Harry Potter films, but they hadn't been released yet. *My Kingdom* was his 75th picture in a long, distinguished, and sometimes controversial career.

Harris strolled into the suite, his flowing white hair topped by a cheekily cocked beret. He wore an old, frayed sweater and held a large Starbucks coffee in one hand. We had an animated conversation about his early film work on the much-talked-about epic remake of *Mutiny on the Bounty* starring Marlon Brando as Fletcher Christian and Harris in a smaller but pivotal role as Mills, the crewman instrumental in inciting the mutiny. "I wasn't even supposed to be in that fooking film," he told me. "Nobody fooking knew who I was, but one actor dropped out at the last minute and my photograph was the next on the pile on the producers' desk, so I was told, 'Right, you're in. Get yourself the fook down to Tahiti.'"

When the official banter ended, Harris lounged around the suite, and I was happy to continue our chat, since he had no other interview before lunch. We talked about hotels and hotel living, shared stories about the various hotels we'd enjoyed in far-off parts of the world, and traded anecdotes about hotels such as the Chelsea in New York, Chateau Marmont in Los

Angeles, the Plaza in New York, the Ritz in Paris, the Royal York in Toronto, and the Savoy in London.

"I used to live in the Savoy, you know," Harris said. I asked him for how long. "Oh, bloody hell, on and off for many years, because I was going from one film location to the other — Tahiti one day, Los Angeles the next, Montana, Mexico, Rome. I found that just being enveloped in the beautiful Savoy to be the most comfortable and convenient thing to do." I told Harris some of my Royal York stories, then the actor chuckled and told me, in true Irish raconteur style, that he had a story for me that perfectly illustrated how comfortable he had been in the Savoy.

In 1970 Harris starred in the revisionist western *A Man Called Horse*. He played an English aristocrat who is captured by Plains Indians in 1825 and must survive the ordeal by using his wits. The movie was a surprise hit, so much so that producer Sandy Howard, in true Hollywood fashion, wanted to make a sequel. "I wasn't averse to the idea of doing the Morgan role again," Harris told me. "It was a great role, but there needed to be some reason other than money to do it." *A Man Called Horse* stayed in theatres for months before going on to become very popular overseas, as well. Then, two years after its initial release, it was re-released in theatres and was a success all over again.

The pressure to make another *A Man Called Horse* film was ratcheted up, and finally in 1975 Howard had such a desire for making the sequel with Harris that he offered the actor a huge salary and the bonus of a Rolls-Royce Silver Shadow. "What I was waiting on really was a good script, a good story, that would be a logical continuation or revisiting of the story," Harris said. "I didn't need a bloody great Rolls-Royce to bribe me into signing. So one day my Rolls-Royce arrives at the Savoy. I didn't know what to do with the fooking thing. I drove it about for a bit, then tossed the keys to the valet fella and asked him to store the bloody thing somewhere."

Harris went off to the American West to make the *Horse* sequel, then journeyed to Italy and France to star in *The Cassandra Crossing*, then to Belgium for *Gulliver's Travels*, then to Malta, California, and Newfoundland to shoot the action adventure *Orca* — movie after movie, location after location. "About 15 years later," he told me, "I was back in my place in the Savoy and someone from the hotel asked me what I wanted done with the item they'd been storing for me all these years. I couldn't for the life of me think what the hell he was on about, so I told him he could do what he wanted with it. It couldn't be all that important, since I couldn't remember a thing about it. Of course, the fella asked me over and over again if I was sure, probably thinking I was drunk or something. Finally, I told the guy he could have whatever this thing was that I stored but had long since forgotten about. There was silence, then the fella said, "But, Mr. Harris, it's a mint-condition Rolls-Royce." For good reason, Richard Harris has a suite named after him at the Savoy.

The Savoy is another one of those iconic, old-world hotels that simply endures. Located on the Strand in Westminster in central London, it was built by the swashbuckling impresario Richard D'Oyly Carte, first opened its doors on August 6, 1889, and quickly gained a reputation as London's most famous hotel. Many people assume the Savoy, with its panoramic views of the Thames River, is a lot larger than it actually is, but it only has 268 rooms. The hotel was erected on land next door to the Savoy Theatre. Carte originally planned to use the site to house a giant electric generator for his theatre, which was the first structure in the world to be fully lit and powered with electricity. The Savoy took just over five years to finish and was financed through Carte's partnership with the wildly successful theatrical team of

Gilbert and Sullivan. It has been said that the success of Gilbert and Sullivan's comic opera *The Mikado* funded the building of the hotel, which itself became the first such establishment with electric lights and elevators.

Over the next few decades the hotel was fought over by greedy partners and traded hands a number of times. It was, like many venerable hotels, the scene of great pomp and ceremony, and great scandal, as well. The hotel figured prominently in the gross indecency trial of Oscar Wilde and was the location of the first ever public sighting of Princess Elizabeth and her future husband, Prince Philip. When Princess Elizabeth became Queen Elizabeth II, her coronation ball was held at the Savoy and was attended by Hollywood stars, political figures, and other notables from around the globe, each paying 12 guineas to attend. French Impressionist Claude Monet and American artist James Whistler both lived in the Savoy

(Courtesy Fairmont Hotels & Resorts)

London, England's luxurious Savoy Hotel was first opened by opera impresario Richard D'Oyly Carte in 1889.

for a while and painted the Thames from their suites. The wild romance of Vivien Leigh and Laurence Olivier started when the pair met at the Savoy. Elizabeth Taylor and Richard Burton once had roaring champagne-fuelled fights there, and when Bob Dylan was living at the Savoy in 1965, he went into a grungy alley adjacent to the Savoy to film his now-famous *Subterranean Homesick Blues*.

More takeover bids and jockeying for ownership followed until 2004 when the Savoy was sold to Saudi businessman Al-Waleed bin Talal to be managed by Fairmont Hotels and Resorts of Toronto. In late 2007 the Savoy closed its doors to undergo a major refit. The makeover was initially supposed to cost £100 million and involve a complete redecoration of the rooms on the Thames riverbank in Edwardian style and the suites on the Strand side in an Art Deco fashion. Butler service would return to the hotel, and chef Gordon Ramsay would preside over the operation of the Savoy Grill. But a monkey wrench was thrown into the plans when it was discovered there were a number of structural problems to be addressed before the ambitious schemes could be implemented, almost doubling the amount the renovations would cost and delaying the reopening significantly. In 2010, however, the Savoy Hotel triumphantly returned to become even more celebrated than ever.

During the writing and editing of the two books I did on Johnny Depp (*Depp* and *Johnny Depp Photo Album*), I interviewed him in hotels, almost always Los Angeles ones, either the Four Seasons in Beverly Hills, the Standard on Sunset Boulevard in West Hollywood, or Chateau Marmont almost directly across the street. Early in his Hollywood career, Depp lived at Chateau Marmont as many other young actors do because it's a hip place, it has history, and it's where the rest of the cool

French Impressionist Claude Monet (1840–1926) was one of the many distinguished residents of London's Savoy Hotel.

Hollywood crowd hangs out. I asked him once about Chateau Marmont. "When you walk into this place," he said, "you don't feel like you're walking into a cathedral or walking into a big bank building. You feel like you're walking into a big old house that belongs to a relative."

When I spoke to actress Winona Ryder, she said it was in "this place," Chateau Marmont, that she and Depp had their first real private conversation and then their first actual date. "We had met earlier in the evening at the popcorn counter at a theatre during the premiere of *Great Balls of Fire*," said Ryder. "Then, at the after-party at Chateau Marmont, we found ourselves in a quiet corner on the terrace overlooking Sunset and just talking about the things we were interested in — common things we loved, like Ennio Morricone's score for *The Mission*. It was like the rest of the party just vanished. We were in kind of dream state. We were two young actors who were working and getting well-known. We were standing on the terrace of one of the most iconic places in Hollywood, with Sunset Boulevard happening below us. There was really something magically surreal about it all."

I asked Depp if that evening was one of his big hotel-living moments, and he said, "Absolutely it was, and for all the right reasons for a change." What Depp was referring to was one of the more notorious incidents involving himself and hotel living. In 1995, after starring in Tim Burton's film *Ed Wood*, Depp was in New York City residing in The Mark, the classy Madison Avenue hotel. He was to begin work soon on a new movie but was obligated to do a few days' worth of publicity duty to promote *Ed Wood*.

Depp isn't a big fan of media junkets in which actors and directors are put in hotel rooms to undergo innumerable five-minute interviews one after the other. Nevertheless, he does them all with a cordiality that has catapulted him to his current place atop the Hollywood heap, but he still doesn't like them. On this particular weekend Depp did dozens of interviews, then went out to blow off steam and have a few drinks with his pals. When he returned to his suite at The Mark quite late, he was tired and annoyed that he had to do more interviews the next day. Depp hung his jacket on the coat rack, and it slid off. He picked it up and put it on the coat rack again, but it slipped off again. In frustration he scooped up the jacket and slammed it onto the coat rack, causing the latter to fall against a large antique mirror on the wall. The mirror was jarred off the wall and crashed onto a table loudly.

A guest in the next suite was awakened rudely by the noise and instantly called down to the front desk to complain. A hotel security man headed up to Depp's suite, and when he arrived, the wrecked mirror frame was resting in the hall and Depp was trying to clean up the broken glass himself. The actor apologized to the security guy, but the man insisted that Depp leave the hotel immediately.

"I remember being dumbfounded," Depp told me. "I'd paid for the suite long in advance, I apologized, I was even helping to clean up. It was all over. And it was, like, two in the morning, where was I going to go?" The security man knew who the actor was and was clearly power-tripping. Depp refused and shut the door. The next knock at the door a half-hour later was by even more insistent New York Police Department officers sent to arrest Depp for causing a disturbance and disorderly conduct. Depp was put in handcuffs and taken to the city's notorious Tombs where he was booked, questioned, and locked up for the evening.

"It was a strange night," Depp said. "One minute I was getting fingerprinted and the next I was in a cell and female cops

were handing me things through the bars for me to autograph."
What made this whole incident even weirder was the identity
of the person in the next suite, the guy who complained about
Depp — none other than Roger Daltrey, the legendary front
man for the notorious hotel-room-destroying British band,
The Who.

When I was working on the first draft of Depp, I was in New
York doing interviews and decided to stop by The Mark and
photograph the door to the suite Depp is now forever wrongly
identified as having trashed. I intended to use the photograph
to illustrate the chapter I was writing about the incident. It was
an extraordinarily hot day when I went up to The Mark's 14th
floor. The maid was in Depp's old suite doing housekeeping
with the door open, so I had to wait until she completed her
chores and the door was closed. As soon as I could, I took a few
photographs of the door with a throwaway camera and headed
for the elevator. On the way down, the elevator stopped on the
tenth floor, a guy in a suit stepped in, and the car continued its
descent. The guy asked me, "Are you a guest in the hotel, sir?
I'm security."

I told him I wasn't a guest in his hotel but was staying down
by Central Park in Essex House. He then asked why I was taking
pictures of their doors. To answer him I explained the whole
Depp research thing. He then said that since I wasn't a guest
I had to leave the hotel. I told him I was on my way out. He
insistently demanded, "Now, sir?" I chuckled, which made him
angry. I explained that we were in an elevator but that when
we landed at the lobby floor and the doors opened, I would
certainly leave. As the doors opened, the security man took my
arm. I made a move to shrug him off, since I was voluntarily
leaving; I didn't need his physical support. While he escorted
me out of the hotel, he snidely mentioned that he was, in fact,

the guy who had gone to Depp's room that night a couple of years earlier, which explained a lot.

My first actual hotel conversation with Johnny Depp occurred when I sat down to interview him in Los Angeles in the early summer of 1997. We were there to talk about his soon-to-be-released rendition of Hunter S. Thompson's character Raoul Duke in *Fear and Loathing in Las Vegas*. I met Depp in a large suite in the Four Seasons Hotel in Beverly Hills; I was in a suite on a lower floor. When I was introduced to Depp, we struck up an instant conversation about Native American history and traditions. He asked if I had any Native in me. I told him I had, but very little. "If I cut myself shaving in the morning," I said, "I've lost most of my Native blood." Depp corrected me and told me that if I had one drop of Native blood in me, I should take great pride in that.

We began to talk about hotels and living in hotels. He talked about his time at Chateau Marmont, and I told him I'd love to live in a hotel someday. "But you got to pick your spot right, man," he said, "or better yet, let the spot pick you." I asked him what he meant by that. He looked around the suite we were in. "See, like, I couldn't live in this place, in this space here, at least not for any length of time. It's just too ... perfect, you know? The colours seem to be arranged so you don't notice any colour at all. There's nothing that's unique about it. I like a hotel to be wearing its character out in the open, like you're living with the place, not just in or at the place." I nodded as if I understood what he meant, and I did comprehend the words he was saying, but it wasn't until recently that I really grasped what he'd meant once I started feeling the same thing myself.

Another accidental hotel connection came from an actor I'd always admired but never had the chance to meet until later in his career, long after his wild-man stage had passed. Dennis

Hopper died at the age of 74 in 2010, and I was saddened at the loss. To me his film *Easy Rider* was one of the landmark pictures in the history of American cinema, and his contributions to the James Dean movies *Rebel Without a Cause* and *Giant* were also a worthy legacy. It wasn't until long after Hopper played the purely evil Frank Booth in David Lynch's brilliant but monstrous *Blue Velvet* that I finally had the good fortune to do two interviews with him over three years.

Still, I'll never forget the first time I laid eyes on him in person. It was a scary moment. I was heading to New York to do a few interviews with Willem Dafoe, Saul Zaentz, and Anthony Minghella, among others, about their film *The English Patient*, but because there was a threatened labour action to shut the roads leading in and out of Pearson International Airport in Toronto, I was advised to go to the airport the evening before. That was the only way I could guarantee being at the airport in time for my early-morning flight. Spending the night in the airport sucked, of course, but I made my flight and fulfilled my commitment to do the interviews.

When I arrived at the Regency Hotel in Manhattan that morning, I was tired and not in the best mood. I just wanted to get to the reception desk and beg them for an early check-in, have a shower, and sleep for a couple of hours before the screening of *The English Patient*. The problem was there was a guy at the reception desk complaining and arguing about every single item on his bill. After 20 minutes or so, I tapped the guy on the shoulder and asked if he might allow me to check in quickly, then resume his battle with the hotel. The guy slowly turned and glared at me. It was Frank Booth! Hopper's lips were tight and his brow furrowed. Then he said softly, "I'm sorry, man. I didn't think anyone was waiting in line. You have to watch these hotels or they'll rob you blind."

I sighed with relief. I had expected to hear a growling Frank Booth repeat his lines from *Blue Velvet*: "I'll send you a love letter straight from my heart, fucker! And do you know what a love letter from me is? A bullet from a fucking gun, fucker!"

Sometime later I finally sat down with Hopper for an interview and lunch outside Chateau Marmont's little restaurant in West Hollywood. He told me he wasn't drinking anymore but that it was all right if I wanted to enjoy a drink in his presence. I told him I never imbibed during the day, only at night and only after my work was finished. For that I got an "Atta boy!" from Hopper. As we chatted about his long and mercurial career, we ended up talking a lot about Chateau Marmont and his varied and checkered experiences there. Two stories he told me have never left me. He confirmed the tale I'd heard about James Dean crashing through the window of Nicholas Ray's bungalow to get a reading for *Rebel Without a Cause*, only Hopper added that Ray, who was 43 at the time, was having a torrid affair with Natalie Wood, who was 17 then.

Hopper idolized Dean, and when the latter died in a car wreck before the film was even released, Hopper told me it was one of the worst days of his life, a day when he almost lost all interest in living himself. Just after the movie was finished and before Dean was due to shoot his next picture (*Giant*, which Hopper also had a small role in), Hopper told me that he, Dean, and Natalie checked into a large suite at Chateau Marmont and decided to celebrate their good fortune by having a rather indulgent, Hollywood-style, good time. They ordered bottle after bottle of champagne from room service and filled the bathtub with it. Wood was the first to undress and climb into the tub. As she splashed around naked in the champagne, her face contorted and she yelped in pain. The acidity of the champagne caused a severe burning sensation in her vagina that quickly became unbearable. "We didn't know what to do," Hopper said. "She was rolling around on the floor with a towel clutched between her legs. We didn't know what happened, so we bundled her up in blankets and got her over to the hospital for treatment."

My next hotel meeting with Hopper was in New York at the elegant Essex House overlooking Central Park. As we settled into his suite, I mentioned that it was at the nearby Regency Hotel that I first laid eyes on him. He said he didn't remember that incident specifically, but it certainly sounded like something he'd done a number of times before. When we finished talking about his new movie, we chatted about hotels for a while. "The thing I really like about living in hotels for long periods of time," he said, "is that everyone's very friendly and protective of you when you're there. You're safe and you're worry free."

Hopper said that one of his most pleasant hotel stints occurred in Hawaii when he was making *Waterworld* with Kevin Costner. He wouldn't tell me which hotel it was (I figured he couldn't remember the actual name) but said: "What was terrific about that place was the inside, the bathroom, the bed, the layout, was all ... hotel. I'd been in similar suites in different places, but there, in Hawaii, you step out on the terrace and you have this paradise before you all around, step inside and you're back in the comfortable familiarity of the suite. That's the beauty of going to nice hotels. It's like taking a comfortable home with you all over the world wherever you go and, you know, the same goes for small, funky little hotels, as well. I've had wonderful times in little hotels out in the middle of nowhere because you're feeling the fun of being somewhere new, but you're living right there, so there's a relaxation and comfort that makes it even more fun."

I had to agree with Hopper on many of his points, and shared with him my story about spending time at the Ritz-Carlton, Kapalua, in Maui. The suites in Ritz-Carlton hotels are very much the same no matter where you are. I'd been in the Ritz-Carlton in Pasadena before that, and it was remarkably similar to the Ritz-Carlton a world away in Maui. The difference, though, was that when you drew the curtains in one, you had the San Gabriel Mountains, but when you parted the curtains in the other, you glimpsed lush Polynesian vegetation, volcanic cliffs, and crashing surf.

During my time in Maui at the Ritz-Carlton, I interviewed people involved with making the film *The Beach*, including Leonardo DiCaprio, Virginie Ledoyen, and Scottish director Danny Boyle. One windy afternoon I took a stroll along a ridge above the beach with Boyle. Everywhere there were beautiful flowers and swaying palm trees. We talked about movies and about Captain James Cook and his crew and what it must have been like to lay eyes on this paradise for the very first time.

Later that afternoon, as the sun began to set, I ventured alone onto a huge lava cliff. A Hawaiian dude, a doorman at the Ritz-Carlton, Kapalua, told me not to get too close to the edge because the waves were high and I could be knocked over and cut up on the jagged volcanic rock or be washed over the edge. I told the dude I'd be careful but that I wanted to see the power of the Pacific Ocean.

As I approached the gaping wound in the side of the cliff, I was amazed at the constant ebb and flow of the waves. Then I noticed a huge swell rolling in. The collision of the wave coming in and the surge going out caused a large gusher to splash upward and crash loudly. Immediately, I noticed another big wave rolling in, with a second one just behind it. Then a mammoth swell tumbled out and was hit by an immense wave heading in. A column of water hurtled straight up for me. I was scared to death! Hunkering down, I grabbed a jutting rock and held on for dear life. I was hit by a wall of water that rocked me sideways, then smacked down on me from above. It pushed me hard against the rock but lasted mere seconds.

When the water receded, leaving puddles around me, I slowly started breathing again. I got up and hustled across the rock floor to the lawn leading to the path back to the Ritz-Carlton. As I passed the Hawaiian doorman I'd encountered earlier, I was literally dripping with water and the inside of my right arm was badly scraped by the jagged rock. The doorman asked, "Are you all right, sir?"

"What's it look like?" I replied.

He chuckled. "I told you, brother, I told you …"

I reached into my pocket, pulled out a sopping wet five-dollar bill, and slapped it in the doorman's hand. "Thanks for the advice, brother. If you have any more for me on anything at all, I'm going to listen this time."

The Ritz-Carlton, Kapalua, in Hawaii's Maui transports its guests to a lush realm of Polynesian vegetation, volcanic cliffs, and crashing surf.

~ ~ ~

While I've always loved hotels and have always had a mystical affair with the Royal York, my devotion turned into a career move about a decade ago when the *Globe and Mail* asked me to write a two-page spread on luxury hotels and the indulgences extended to celebrities in those establishments. I thought that would be fun, so I happily accepted. One of the hotels I chose to feature was Raffles L'Ermitage in Beverly Hills, a place movie stars love because it seems secluded even though it's between West Hollywood and Rodeo Drive.

One weekend Eddie Murphy stayed at L'Ermitage with his children, so he asked the hotel to install a sandbox, a jungle gym, and other diversions for kids on the pool level. The hotel did as he instructed (and paid for). Murphy and his children were in the hotel for only one night. That evening a very popular boy band was staying in a cluster of suites on the same floor. The marijuana smoke emanating from their rooms was so thick and constant that the hotel had to install stand-up fans in the halls to disperse it.

One of my strangest hotel experiences occurred in L'Ermitage. I was in Los Angeles to interview Jodie Foster and Chow Yun Fat about their film *Anna and the King*. After a delightful afternoon talking to Chow Yun Fat, who helped me out with my book *Ten Thousand Bullets* about his frequent collaborator director John Woo, I was relaxing in my suite, listening to Nina Simone's song "Sinner Man," and making notes for the interview I had to do the next day with Jodie Foster. Suddenly, there was a knock on the door. I opened it without peering through the peephole, since it wasn't unusual for the movie studio hosting the interviews to send a bottle of wine or snacks up to the suites.

On the other side of the door was a naked young woman. She was in her late twenties and on the short side, but she was built like a personal trainer. The lady looked embarrassed and was using her arms to cover herself. I was taken aback. Even in Los Angeles this was something else. I needed time to process what was happening. Then she said, "I'm really sorry. My asshole boyfriend threw me out of his suite. Can I borrow a robe?"

I stepped aside and allowed her in, casting a lingering glance at her rear view as she strolled into my suite. Shaking my head, I averted my eyes, got a robe from the bathroom, and brought it to her. She wrapped herself in it and stood there awkwardly. I asked her if she needed to use the phone. She said no, that her boyfriend would cool down in a few minutes and it would be okay. The woman had barely gotten those words out when there was another knock on the door. We both headed for the door. When I opened it, I was confronted with a well-known young Irish actor with a reputation as a bad boy.

"Sorry, mate," the Irish actor said. "Sorry about the disturbance."

I told him not to mention it, that up until now the evening had been rather dull. The woman spoke quietly to the actor, then slipped out of my suite.

My Irish "pal" chuckled. "Well, you get what you pay for, I guess. Sorry again." He then swaggered back across the hall.

A couple of hours later, around 11:00 p.m., I was watching an old film on Turner Classic Movies when there was yet another rap on the door. I opened it, and there was the Irish actor again. He handed me back my robe and a nice bottle of Glenfiddich Scotch. "For your troubles …"

I took the bottle and robe, thanked him, and asked if everything was okay.

"Like I was tellin' you before. You get what you fooking pay for. Never a truer truism than that, mate."

Awkward moments with famous folk are legion when the setting is the comfort of a hotel. On two occasions my discomfort turned to bemused wonder. The first happened when I was sent to Los Angeles to interview the Canadian actor Ryan Gosling. I had met Gosling before in Toronto during the Toronto International Film Festival. Our encounter this time took place in the Standard Hotel on Sunset Boulevard in West Hollywood. The Standard is one of those precious Hollywood hipster hangouts. Its name hangs upside down for some reason, and its suites are full of colourful furnishings and bean bag chairs, making the place seem like an upscale version of an early 1970s hotel.

I arrived at the appointed time and headed into the lounge to meet Gosling. No one was in the bar when I arrived except a bartender, a waitress, and Gosling, who was in a dark corner of the place. But the actor wasn't alone. He was with a lady friend. They were wrapped around each other, kissing and groping as if there were no tomorrow. I stood there uneasily for a moment. Gosling was pretty busy, so he didn't notice me. I took a seat at the bar, my back to the Ryan Gosling Live Sex Show. The bartender came over to me, I ordered a drink, then told him I was supposed to meet the guy at the table behind me but didn't want to disturb the man until his current scene ran its natural course. Smiling, I asked the bartender to tell me when the two lovebirds came up for air.

After 15 minutes or so, the bartender told me it looked as if the liplock was over. I quickly swivelled off the stool and headed to Gosling's table, only to be surprised to see that the actor's lady friend was Sandra Bullock. Back then Bullock was 38 and Gosling was 23. Bullock said hello to me, excused herself, and strutted out of the lounge. I sat with Gosling and had a wonderful conversation, both of us drinking a bit more than we should have.

Sometime later I had a second intriguing encounter with famous folk when I ran into Bullock again, this time on my home turf at the Royal York in September 2006 during the Toronto International Film Festival. That morning I'd seen *Infamous*, the film Bullock was promoting at the festival, in which she plays a supporting role as Harper Lee, the author of *To Kill a Mockingbird*. I went into the Library Bar to meet someone else and was quite early, so I thought I'd make some notes at a quiet table in the corner. To my delight, Bullock was sitting at the table next to mine.

She had a glass of wine in front of her, a cellphone, and a day planner. Having been a celebrity interviewer for more than a decade by that time, I knew the protocol and how to read certain signals and body language. I could tell when someone didn't want to be bothered or approached, and I almost always respected my instincts, but I admired Bullock's performance so much that I wanted to tell her as much, then go back to my business and allow her to return to hers.

"Excuse me, Ms. Bullock," I said. "I saw *Infamous* this morning and wanted to tell you I thought it was probably the best thing I've ever seen you do."

She looked at me with that beautiful, infectious smile of hers and thanked me, then asked, "Were there a lot of people at the screening?"

I told her it was at a smaller cinema but that it had been packed.

"And how did the film go over, generally speaking?"

I said everyone had been riveted and that there was a spontaneous outburst of applause over the end titles. She treated me to another beaming smile. We then engaged in a casual conversation about the film festival and about the Library Bar itself. I told her that it was a famous place within an even more renowned establishment and gave her a brief history of the hotel. Bullock finished her wine and wanted another, so rather than wave or call out, she got up and headed over to request another glass from the waitress. She asked me if I wanted another cognac on her, as well. I thanked her and said I'd love that.

When she ordered the drinks from the waitress, she was recognized by fans in the bar and was asked for her autograph. Patiently, she signed every autograph and posed for a few hastily snapped pictures. Bullock returned to her table, and our new drinks arrived soon after. Sipping some wine, she smiled at me. "One guy asked me to sign an autograph and told me he loved me in *My Cousin Vinny*. Then he handed me a Canadian five-dollar bill to sign."

I asked her what she'd done, since I knew she wasn't in *My Cousin Vinny*; Marisa Tomei was.

"I signed it for him, but I signed Marisa Tomei because I didn't want to shatter his illusion."

One of my fondest memories of a stay in a hotel occurred when I was in Barbados shooting a television pilot. The show was tentatively titled *Admit One* and looked at the reality behind the places, stories, and people featured in blockbuster movies. The pilot focused on *Pirates of the Caribbean*. We were in a place where many real pirates had lived, hidden out, and done their nefarious business. The first episode was shot on a sloop roughly the size of a pirate ship, just outside the home of the legendary Sam Lord, an actual early-19th-century pirate who was something of a lazy bugger. He strung lanterns on the reef offshore from his house. Cargo ships and merchant vessels spotted the lanterns, mistook them for a harbour, crashed on the reef, and became disabled. Lord and his crew then sallied out and robbed them blind before the ships sank.

After shooting on the water all day, my producer/cameraman Mike MacKinnon and I went for dinner at the Fairmont Royal Pavilion Hotel. The host for the evening was the delightful Alpha Jackman, one of the managers there at the time. He was informed ahead of time that we were coming and that I was a lover of hotels and would probably write about his hotel when I got home, so we were given special treatment. As we ate our seafood dinner, Jackman revealed that he was called Alpha because he was the first-born in the family and his parents figured they would name each subsequent child after letters in the Greek alphabet. After dinner we talked about rum, one of Barbados's great exports. I told Alpha I wasn't an expert on rum but did tend to drink only it while in his country. He said that rum was more than just a drink; it was part of the island nation's culture and heritage. I didn't dispute that in the least but confessed I probably couldn't tell one brand or vintage of rum from another no matter how immersed in the stuff I was.

Alpha insisted that I could tell the difference if I was given the proper education, if I was indoctrinated into the world of rum by a rum lover and expert. He then arranged for a private rum-tasting event right then and there at our table. Before I knew it at least ten glasses of rum were in front of each of us — Mount Gay, Old Brigand, Cockspur, Barbados Rum. The first glass slid to us was Mount Gay. Alpha told us that having first been created in Barbados in 1703 it was the oldest and finest brand of rum on the planet.

As we sipped the alcohol, we were given a fabulous history lesson by the passionate Jackman. We scarcely realized we were steadily making our way through ten glasses of straight rum. While the event was ongoing, I felt fine. I was fascinated by Jackman's love of the culture and history of the various brands of rum, something I would never have been exposed to were it not for this convergence of events.

When it was time to retire for the evening, I was finally feeling the effects of all that rum. I could walk, but I had to concentrate hard on each step and where to place my feet and was grateful to the Royal Pavilion for its decision to illuminate the laneways with lights on the ground and in the trees. As I lay in bed that night, I chuckled ruefully in dread of what I would feel like in the morning. The next day, though, I felt reasonably okay. My head seemed like a coconut, big, thick, with liquid sloshing around inside, but I wasn't suffering from a hangover.

Later, when I ran into Jackman in the beach area behind the hotel, I mentioned that I was surprised I had no hangover. He looked almost as if I'd insulted him and said, "You only get a hangover from cheap rum, man, from not so good rum from someplace else, man, not from de finest rum in de world."

I humbly apologized for my oversight.

During a hotel trip to northern Italy, I had another alcohol-related incident that was as interesting as the Barbados experience but in a much different fashion. I was in Italy to write about the little seaside and countryside hotels in places like San Remo, Portofino, Ventimiglia, and Cinque Terra. In Ventimiglia I lived in Hotel Sole Mare, a quaint, bright seaside place. The people were extraordinarily friendly, and the food in the restaurant was wonderful (*pasta e basta* — pasta and nothing else!). One night I took a stroll along the beach and stopped at a little bar that seemed populated by local people. I went in for a drink to soak up more of the rich atmosphere around me and noticed something high up on a shelf behind the bar — a dusty bottle of absinthe.

Absinthe has a fascinating history. It was actually used by the French in the First World War as an anaesthetic because it is so powerful (as much as 75 percent alcohol), has an anise-like taste that's smoothly pleasant, and contains the herb wormwood, which in turn has a chemical called thujone that reputedly sends you soaring even higher. It was once a potent and cheap drink, so artists and peasants adored it. Oscar Wilde actually loved it to death. Vincent van Gogh had a glass of absinthe on the table the night he cut off part of his ear. Edgar Allan Poe was also a big fan.

Because absinthe was so strong, there were recorded incidents of people committing multiple murders under its influence, so French wine producers, who saw their profits eroded significantly by this cheap spirit, banded together and got absinthe banned as a hazardous menace to societal order and well-being. Absinthe was illegal for a long time in many European nations and in North America, though it was never banned in Spain and Portugal. Recently, an absinthe revival started, and laws were changed to allow the spirit to be sold and produced in several European countries such as France, Holland, the Czech Republic, and Britain. Even in the United States and Canada it is now legal.

I first tried absinthe a few years before my trip to Italy. I was with Johnny Depp in West Hollywood at Chateau Marmont when he had a few bottles sent to him from Britain. It was the real stuff, so I did know something about the spirit and was aware of the effect it could have. I asked the bartender, an Italian woman in her sixties, for an absinthe and pointed to the dusty bottle on the shelf. She looked at me and asked, "Are you sure?" in Italian. Not being able to speak the language, I assumed that was what she said based on her facial expression. For all I knew, she might have said, "Are you nuts?" In any event I answered yes.

The woman hauled the bottle down and knew exactly how to prepare the drink. She produced the right kind of glass, dug up a real absinthe spoon from under the bar somewhere, and poured the emerald-green absinthe into the glass. Then she placed the absinthe spoon over the glass, positioned a sugar cube on the spoon, poured the correct amount of water over the cube, and let the water seep through the tiny openings in the spoon until the cube slowly dissolved. After that she slid the glass to me, and I laid some euros on her.

When the sugar cube was nicely dissolved, I used the absinthe spoon to stir it into the drink, transforming it into a rich shade of creamy jade. The first sip of real absinthe goes down with a slight burn, but subsequent sips are dominated by strong sensations of taste and a lovely, powerful aroma. When you ask for an absinthe in a bar like that Italian one, it's a glassful; it isn't a little splash. So one glass of absinthe is enough for me. Paul Gauguin and Vincent van Gogh, though, could knock them back all night.

As I finished my glass of absinthe, I didn't feel drunk or high. I was actually making notes about the place and the experience. The bartender took my empty glass and then a couple of minutes later put another absinthe in front of me. I looked at her quizzically and waved it off, telling her I hadn't asked for another. She laughed and in broken English told me this one was on her. She then pointed at my shirt, which bore the crest of AS Roma, my favourite Italian soccer team. The bartender, too, was a Roma fan. Lucky me.

I began sipping my second absinthe and got about half-way through it, then stopped. I had to be up relatively early in the morning to meet my guide and continue my northern Italy adventure. I remember shaking hands with the bartender, exchanging smiles with her, and thanking her in my version of Italian. I recall the walk back to Hotel Sole Mare and going to bed, even watching a bit of BBC news. However, when I woke up the next morning, it was as if the absinthe had temporarily erased part of my hard drive. I looked around my lovely suite and didn't know where I was, not even which country I was in. Going to the window, I opened the curtains to a beautiful seaside vista and thought, *Wherever I am, it sure is beautiful!*

Perhaps I'm in the south of France, I thought. After all, I had a vague recollection of being on an Air France plane. A little concerned now, I went to the desk and took out some hotel stationery that identified Hotel Sole Mare in Ventimiglia, Italy. At that point my memories all came flooding back with a clarity and purity that shocked me even more. I swore off absinthe forever that day. Later, however, I was approached by a British absinthe distiller to write the above story for a page on its website. My fee for writing the story was a big bottle of absinthe!

Drinking in hotel bars is something else writers and actors who live in hotels tend to do more of than the average person. It's like having a wonderful, comfortable, familiar bar in your basement. You can drink and relax and home is just upstairs; you don't have to venture out or drive anywhere. This subject came up in an interview I did with Canadian actor Michael J. Fox, who is one of the most down-to-earth superstars I've ever met. Fox lived in the penthouse of a Florida hotel for a long time when he was shooting *Doc Hollywood* and found the bar downstairs much to his liking.

"I was drinking too much at the time," Fox told me. "It was a very interesting, almost surreal time for me. I was enjoying a lot of success on TV and in movies, so I was almost feeling guilty about being on the receiving end of too much good fortune. I was living in this big hotel in Florida, and they had me in the penthouse, which was huge. I think that was part of the problem. It was too big. It was like living in a ballroom. So in the evenings after work, or on the days off, I'd hang out in the bar, which felt more intimate and comfortable and I could talk to people and enjoy myself, then simply ride the elevator to the warehouse-sized suite I was living in. After a couple of months of that, I found that I was actually staying in the bar until it closed. On the one hand, it was a very positive experience because I would be mixing and socializing with people who lived real and varied lives. I really needed exposure to them at that time."

In the Royal York, just off the escalator leading from the lobby to the mezzanine, is York Station, a little bar tucked away in the corner. It's the smallest bar in Toronto and at full capacity holds only 16 people. Anyone who has ever had a drink there will say it's the comfiest bar they've ever relaxed in, a sentiment I can echo most loudly.

Sometimes a hotel bar isn't a good place to meet a celebrity for an interview. Once, I spent a lazy, rainy afternoon in the bar of the Nelligan, a lovely Old Montreal hotel named after Émile Nelligan, the noted Quebec poet. I was there sipping drinks with Edward Norton and having a free-ranging, engaging conversation. Norton is a fine actor, proof of which comes from his Academy Award nominations for his first film (*Primal Fear*) and his fifth picture (*American History X*). He was in Montreal shooting a lively but uneven heist drama called *The Score*. Part of the reason he wanted to be in this film so badly was the fact that his two co-stars were Marlon Brando and Robert De Niro.

What was unique about *The Score* was that it was actually written to be set in Boston and was being shot in Montreal to save money. However, when director Frank Oz went to Montreal to scout locations, he found the city not only charming but dynamic and a bit exotic, as well. So he had the screenplay revised to be set in Montreal, which ultimately saved the production even more money since the sets didn't have to be dressed up to look like American streets with U.S. mailboxes and flags and Boston police cars everywhere.

Norton and I were having a great conversation about living in hotels. I told him about staying in the nearby Fairmont Queen Elizabeth Hotel and living for a while in what is called the John Lennon Suite, since that was where John and Yoko Ono staged their Bed-In for Peace and wrote and recorded "Give Peace a Chance." Our conversation was lively and smart. Norton is a smart guy and likes to engage other people he perceives to be intelligent. But he's also a movie star, which means he has a healthy ego. Just as our conversation was winding down, a young woman sheepishly approached the table and said, "Excuse me ..."

We both glanced up and smiled at her, assuming she was going to compliment Norton and ask him to sign something. Instead she extended a hand to me and said, "You're the guy from the show *Reel to Real*, aren't you? You guys are wonderful. I never miss a show. I just wanted to tell you that. Sorry for interrupting."

She walked out of the bar, and I uncomfortably smiled at Norton, who looked a bit dour. The rest of our chat was strained and sharp, and we parted company a few minutes later.

But let's return to the aforementioned John Lennon Suite. Le Reine Élizabeth, or as it's known today in English, Fairmont The Queen Elizabeth, is an iconic hotel in Montreal like Toronto's Royal York. Both were originally created as railway hotels (the Royal York by Canadian Pacific and the Queen Elizabeth by Canadian National Railways), both are connected to train stations, and both have fascinating histories. Hard-core Quebec nationalists wanted the big hotel in the centre of town to be called Château Maisonneuve after Paul Chomedey de Maisonneuve, the man credited as the founder of Montreal, but since Queen Elizabeth II had just taken the throne in 1952 when the hotel was being designed, CN boss Donald Gordon decided to christen it Le Reine Élizabeth, which struck some as odd because of the use of *Le*, a masculine article. However, the article actually refers to the hotel, not to Elizabeth.

The Queen Elizabeth gained worldwide attention on May 26, 1969, when John Lennon and Yoko Ono took over the large, comfortable suite 1742 and rearranged it hippie style so they could stage their Bed-In for Peace — a peaceful, wacky protest against the war in Vietnam. Actually, the Queen Elizabeth wasn't the first choice for John and Yoko. They were heading to New York where they thought their peace protest would get the attention of the United Nations, but the pair were denied entry into the United States. So they picked Montreal because John liked what he'd been reading about Pierre Elliott Trudeau, Canada's charismatic French-Canadian prime minister.

Over the next several days they lay around in bed, did press conferences, gave interviews in their pajamas, ordered room service, played music, and entertained a suite full of guests who included everyone from Trudeau to LSD guru Timothy Leary. They also wrote and hastily recorded "Give Peace a Chance" on rudimentary equipment. Despite what many people think, the

Montreal's Queen Elizabeth Hotel has had many famous guests, but perhaps John Lennon and Yoko Ono are the most celebrated ones, thanks to their attention-grabbing Bed-In for Peace in 1969.

session wasn't an improvised jam. The lyrics of the song were John Lennon's, penned on a few handwritten sheets of paper, and the recording included anyone who was in the room at the time of the various takes. All were invited to sing along with that now-famous chorus: "All we are saying is give peace a chance."

Suite 1742 was restored to its previous state after the Lennon and Ono flying circus left town, with the bed returned to the bedroom from the living room where the couple had moved it. The Queen Elizabeth's management later decided to promote the "happening" as a historical moment of cool, renaming the rooms the John Lennon Suite and decorating them with a tasteful display of photos and mementos from the event, including framed handwritten lyrics and dinner menu requests. Whenever I stay in the Queen Elizabeth, it's as if Lennon's song, and the energy behind it, permeates the walls of the place.

Montreal probably has the most interesting hotel landscapes in Canada. There are two different kinds of hotels in the city: the big hotels downtown and the boutique hotels in Vieux-Port or Old Montreal. Many of the fine hotels in the older part of town are built into already existing ancient warehouses or foundries, and the Province of Quebec and the City of Montreal have strict regulations on what can be built there or what can be reconstructed. Every building must, by law, maintain the integrity of the historical atmosphere of the area. Even if you are planning to erect a new hotel on property that has no structure already on it, you have to make your newly constructed building appear as if it has stood for hundreds of years.

One of the premier hoteliers in Old Montreal is Dimitri Antonopoulos, who owns four boutique hotels within a few blocks of one another. They range from the hip, luxurious Nelligan and Place d'Armes to the inn-like Auberge du Vieux-Port and the newest addition, Le Petit Hôtel. I once spoke to Dimitri over drinks on the lovely rooftop lounge/restaurant of Le Place d'Armes Hôtel about the challenges for a hotelier in Vieux-Port. "Well, there are challenges of course," he said. "The laws, the bylaws, the various kinds of permissions and inspections that are involved. But ultimately, if you're smart, you make all that work to your advantage. When we were building the Nelligan, we had a very old structure that we had to gut, then retrofit from the inside completely while maintaining the integrity of the exterior of the building, as well. So it's not really about the exterior for us, not entirely. The challenge for us is to make these buildings, some of which have stood here since the late 1600s, early 1700s, into viable living spaces for contemporary and commercial use. It's a very careful and meticulous process."

I asked Dimitri to clarify what he meant by saying that smart hoteliers make the Vieux-Port restrictions work to their advantage. "What I meant by that was simply that since you know these rules, and laws exist, it gives you the opportunity to create very unique hotels in very unique spaces. Instead of trying to conceal the antiquity of the building, you use it and make the hotel as aesthetically interesting as you can by making the best use of what you have. How you decorate and furnish the hotel is up to you, of course, but what the structure ends up being is a partnership between you and history, between you and those who originally built the building however many hundreds of years ago." I then asked him why someone chooses to be a hotelier. "Of course," he said, "I can only speak for myself as to the reasons for that. I've always loved being in nice hotels, so I thought it would be very cool to build the kind of hotels I'd most prefer to stay in, to hang out in myself."

While the Queen Elizabeth is my favourite of the big downtown Montreal hotels and is the one I've spent the most time in, the Ritz-Carlton is a close second in my affections. When a Montreal dreamer, Charles Hosmer, decided to build a hotel like the one his best friend, César Ritz, had opened in Paris, he wanted to use the famous hotelier's name for the establishment. Ritz told Hosmer that he would have to live up to the high standards of his hotel in Paris, which meant a bathroom in every room and a kitchen on each floor so that room service meals could be made as freshly as possible and served course by course. The Parisian also insisted on round-the-clock valet and concierge services and a lobby that was small and intimate but had a grand staircase somewhere in the entranceway.

The $3 million Ritz-Carlton Montreal debuted on December 31, 1912, and began receiving guests at 11:15 p.m. for a lavish ball that lasted until the early-morning hours. The first superstar residents of the Ritz-Carlton Montreal were the silent film star couple Mary Pickford and Douglas Fairbanks.

When the story hit the newspapers that Fairbanks and Pickford were in the hotel, the sidewalks around the Ritz-Carlton were constantly jammed with fans day and night, hoping to catch even a glimpse of the pair. A couple of times per day Fairbanks climbed out onto a balcony above the front sidewalk and waved to the crowds, who screamed loudly before he disappeared back inside.

In 1957 the Ritz-Carlton added 67 rooms and suites. Care was taken not to alter the Louis XVI/Regency ambience and style of the hotel, a policy that remained in place until 1970 when it was felt an overhaul was long overdue. A $3 million facelift was undertaken to transform the Ritz-Carlton from a sort of private club catering to Montreal old money into a new kind of hotel that celebrated its luxury and history while upgrading all services and decor to reflect new tastes in a changing society. The facelift was done slowly and wasn't completed until 1979. By then the costs had doubled to $6 million.

Later, in 1992, the Ritz-Carlton was sold to the European-based Kempinski group of five-star hotels and became an independently managed hotel that operated, quite sensibly, under the old Ritz-Carlton banner. For 15 years it remained the historic landmark it had been for almost 100 years. In late 2006 the Ritz-Carlton was again sold to a consortium that included a subsidiary of the Monaco Luxury Hotels and Resorts group. Plans were almost immediately put in place to gut the hotel and remake it from the inside out, reducing the number of rooms and suites by almost half and replacing them with luxury condo suites and residences. The hotel has completely betrayed what it once was with this transformation. No longer will it be *La Grande Dame*, the Ritz-Carlton of old. Instead it is now one of those new breed of hotels that are nothing more than condo developments with a few hotel-style rooms, the focus shifting from taking care of guests to making sure suite owners are happy.

Two fellow hotel residents I most identify with are *Lolita* author Vladimir Nabokov and hard-boiled U.S. novelist Cornell Woolrich. The former lived in hotels most of his adulthood both when he settled in the United States and for the last 17 years of his life when he resided in Switzerland's Fairmont Montreux Palace. Nabokov said when asked about his choice of accommodation: "Living in a hotel eliminates the nuisance of private ownership and a hotel life confirms me in my favourite habit — the habit of freedom."

Because of the nature of hotels big and small, those who choose to live in them have a set of neighbours that changes a couple of times per week, which means they get to know maids, doormen, and health club attendants much better than most individuals do and find themselves being extraordinary grateful to these people above all others in the hotel hierarchy since the staff are the ones who literally take care of them daily. Around the Montreux Palace, Nabokov was renowned for his kindness and generosity. The staff knew him as a playful and cheerful man who always had time to speak to them and took an interest in who they were and what they did. Many staff members were dumbfounded at the Russian writer's reputation for being aloof and remote.

My experience with the working staff of the Royal York reflects a similar comfort level. One of the people I am in constant, almost daily contact with is Josh Stone, who works at the health club front desk. He is a charming, charismatic fellow who is friendly and unassuming with everyone who comes through the door and is courteous and helpful no matter how rudely or strangely the guest treats him.

Author Vladimir Nabokov (1899–1977) once commented: "Living in a hotel eliminates the nuisance of private ownership and a hotel life confirms me in my favourite habit — the habit of freedom."

After seeing me every morning for months, Josh finally introduced himself and began the much-appreciated habit of laying out a robe and my newspaper on my preferred chair every morning before I arrived for my swim. When I finish swimming, I generally converse with him about movies and my experiences in television. (Josh is an aspiring sketch comedian and actor, and having seen samples of his work, I have to say he has a legitimate shot.) After many of these talks on life, liberty, and the pursuit of happiness, I was surprised and touched to come down a couple days after my birthday for a swim with my lady friend Rhonda to find Josh had set the small table by my chair with a tablecloth, flowers, and a little cheesecake with HAPPY BIRTHDAY written in chocolate on it. When Rhonda and I came out of the pool, Josh arranged for coffee and a Tim Hortons sausage breakfast sandwich on a biscuit for both of us. As Rhonda and I sat and talked in the lounge area, Josh brought out another treat — a lovely bottle of Hennessey Black cognac as a gift. It was a wonderful and memorable gesture from a guy I consider a good friend, not just a pool attendant.

A similar incident happened during the 2010 FIFA World Cup. Coca-Cola was selling gimmick bottles of its beverage shaped like soccer balls. I had a number of them around my suite. One day a favourite maid of mine, with the delightful name of Cassiopeia, asked me where I'd found those promotional bottles of Coke. I told her where I'd gotten them, and a few hours later when I was at that very store, I picked up a bagful for her and made sure she had the soccer bottles before leaving that day. She was very thankful and offered up a big smile. I told her I was happy to do it. Two days later I discovered a fruit plate and a lovely bottle of wine in my suite with a thank-you note from Cassiopeia. When you live in a hotel, you quickly develop a natural friendship with the people you see every day, and it doesn't matter who they are or what they do, because you are all under the same roof.

Nabokov lived in a few different hotels, but it was the Montreux Palace he chose to stay in the last 17 years of his life. However, he wasn't the only writer to pick Montreux as a place to reside. Leo Tolstoy and Lord Byron lived in the town on the shore of Lake Geneva overlooking the Alps, as did composers Pyotr Ilyich Tchaikovsky and Igor Stravinsky. The Montreux Palace itself was built in 1906 and has been a preference of many contemporary musicians (partly attributable to the proximity of the nearby Montreux Jazz Festival). Freddie Mercury of Queen was there so often that one of the suites was named after him. Frank Zappa loved the Montreux Palace and often tore up the joint, including one evening when he set fire to the hotel's casino, which in turn inspired Deep Purple's "Smoke on the Water," one of the most famous rock tunes of all time. Apparently, the members of Deep Purple were watching the flames and smoke wafting over Lake Geneva.

As with the origins of most classic hotels that endure, the birth of the Montreux Palace harks back to a visionary swashbuckler, in this case two Swiss entrepreneurs. Alexandre Emery and Ami Chessex purchased an existing hotel in the Montreux area, the Hôtel du Cygne, and a neighbouring property, then brought in Swiss architect Eugene Jost and asked him to build a palace joined to the original hotel by a *salon de musique*. Jost was instructed to make the new palace as modern as any existing at the time, and he delivered just that in less than 18 months. When the Montreux Palace opened on March 19, 1906, it had private bathrooms in each room, hot and cold running water, electricity, and heated rooms. More than 200 years later, in 2008, the Montreux Palace was given a makeover. The rooms were redecorated, and an emphasis was placed on the space and light afforded by the uninterrupted vistas of Lake Geneva.

I'm a lifelong fan of hard-boiled crime fiction, especially the work of Raymond Chandler, James M. Cain, Jim Thompson, and Cornell Woolrich, who is a personal favourite. Woolrich wrote the story "It Had to Be Murder," which Alfred Hitchcock based his film *Rear Window* on, and numerous other Woolrich novels and stories served as the inspiration for movies ranging from John Farrow's *Night Has a Thousand Faces* to François Truffaut's *The Bride Wore Black*. I recall reading *First You Dream, Then You Die*, Francis M. Nevins, Jr.'s biography of Woolrich, when I was quite young. Even before reading the Woolrich biography I'd dreamed about living a literary life in a big old hotel. Nevins's book only deepened that ambition, since Woolrich details lovingly his many years living in New York City establishments such as Hotel Marseilles, the decrepit Hotel Franconia, and later, finally, the more luxurious Sheraton Russell. The one thing that sticks in my mind among Woolrich's utterances is what the man said about hotel living: "It is a place you can be famous and anonymous at the same time."

What happened at the Montreux Palace with Frank Zappa reminds me of the kind of havoc wreaked by rock bands on

(Courtesy Fairmont Hotels & Resorts)

Switzerland's Montreux Palace Hotel first opened its doors in 1906. Since then it has housed everyone from Vladimir Nabokov to Frank Zappa.

hotel rooms in the late 1960s and early 1970s when such behaviour seemed like a rite of passage. I never could figure out what the late drummer Keith Moon of The Who got out of unplugging the television in his suite and throwing it out the window into the swimming pool, or what the members of Led Zeppelin, who were also fond of the Montreux Palace, derived out of riding motorcycles through the lobby and lounge of Chateau Marmont. And there is a Hyatt hotel on Sunset Boulevard that became such a darling of touring bands because of its proximity to places like Whisky a Go-Go that it was affectionately dubbed the "Riot Hyatt" for years.

In the summer of 1997 the band Oasis was in New York City to plug the release of its then new album *Be Here Now*, the follow-up to the smash LP *(What's the Story) Morning Glory?* I was invited to interview band leaders Noel and Liam Gallagher at the Rhiga Royal Hotel in Manhattan. When I arrived at the Rhiga Royal, I was surprised to see the Gallaghers in the lobby lounge with a record company PR woman. I identified myself as being from the Canadian show the brothers were to be featured on and was asked to sit and wait with them.

The conversation started out cordially. We talked about how big and impressive New York was, Liam and I compared watches, then Noel said something to Liam that I couldn't understand because of his accent. Liam got quite angry, and a loud and profane argument ensued. Next Liam stood abruptly and knocked over the table and our drinks. Then he loomed over Noel as if he were about to begin hammering his brother.

I saw the horror on the face of the young PR person and spotted a hotel security man heading our way. Thinking I should try to diffuse the situation in the interest of saving the interview for my show, I got to my feet next to Liam and suggested, "Maybe we should all calm down a bit."

Liam swung around to me and snapped, "Maybe we should all just mind our own fooking business, eh?" He then pushed a finger into my chest hard enough to knock me off balance and back into my seat. After that he shouted at Noel, "Right, then, I'm going to the fooking pub!"

Noel waved him off and yelled, "Go to the fooking pub! You got nothing to fooking say of any value, anyway."

Liam stormed off, shoved a waiter aside, and slammed the glass door on his way out so hard that we all thought it would shatter.

Later, in a suite on one of the higher floors of the Rhiga Royal, I was told it would only be Noel who would do the interview. He strolled into the suite and shook hands with everyone — crew, producer, host — then came over and shook my hand with a smile. "Nice to see you again, mate. We have to take up that chat we were having about the Premiership [English soccer league] after this is done." He went on to give an interesting interview with no mention of his brother or the commotion they had caused in the hotel lounge. To him it was just another day in the life of a touring rock band, I suppose.

Yousuf Karsh, one of Canada's most famous photographers, chose to live and to create in a hotel, in his case, Ottawa's Fairmont Château Laurier. Like Toronto's Royal York and Montreal's Queen Elizabeth, Château Laurier was established as a railway hotel. Under the direction of the Grand Trunk Railway's chairman Charles Melville Hays, the Château was built in conjunction with Ottawa's Union Station (now the Government Conference Centre). However, the creation of the Château was fraught with problems. Originally, there was a lot of resistance to the project because the chosen site was part of the capital city's Major's Hill Park.

Prime Minister Sir Wilfrid Laurier personally interceded to secure the exact location Hays wanted for his hotel, and because of that, the place was named after him. When plans began to take shape under the guidance of New York architect Bradford Gilbert, Grand Trunk Railway executives quickly took exception to the direction Gilbert was heading in. They felt his scheme didn't reflect the grandness they wanted the hotel to have and found his designs too ordinary. So Gilbert was replaced by the Montreal architectural firm of Ross and MacFarlane. The Château opened on April 26, 1912, and Wilfrid Laurier was there for the inauguration. In 1923 Canadian Pacific Railway bought the Grand Trunk Railway, and the Château became part of CPR's family of hotels. In 1930, when R.B. Bennett was elected prime minister of Canada, he decided

(Courtesy Fairmont Hotels & Resorts)

Ottawa's Château Laurier debuted in 1912 as one of the country's premier railway hotels. Today it sits majestically at the intersection of the Rideau Canal and the Ottawa River.

to live in the Château during his time in office (until 1935). For 60 years, from 1924 until 2004, the Canadian Broadcasting Corporation's English- and French-language radio operations were housed on the sixth floor of the Château.

Like the Savoy in London, the Château looks a lot bigger than it actually is. The hotel has 429 rooms and suites but appears to contain twice that number. I've spent extensive periods in the Château, on both occasions to interview political figures for television. Each time I was in the same suite and loved the place for its high ceilings and oddly configured floor space. As with a lot of rooms in old hotels, the bathroom is right inside the entrance door, but my particular suite had floor space like an abstract square — wide on one side and narrowing to the opposite wall where the credenza containing the TV and the chest of drawers was located. And there were huge windows with tall sets of drapes that made me feel as if I really were living in an old château.

There is a small hotel in Toronto tucked away on Sherbourne Street just south of Bloor Street. From outside it looks like a well-kept Victorian mansion, and that's essentially what it is. It's called the Clarion Hotel & Suites Selby. Many years ago, before it was a hotel, it was the family home of the Gooderhams, Toronto's premier alcohol barons, who built the place in the 1880s. In the early 20th century the family sold the mansion, and it served as the temporary home of Branksome Hall, an exclusive all-girls' school. By 1915 it was transformed into a residential hotel.

In the early 1920s, when Ernest Hemingway worked as a reporter for the *Toronto Star*, he and his wife, Hadley, lived for a time in the residential hotel, then known as the Selby. While working on his newspaper assignments, Hemingway reputedly wrote notes and parts of the early first draft of his novel *A Farewell to Arms*. The hotel, of course, has designated Hemingway's former suite the Hemingway Room and boasts that the author's desk is still there. Curiously, however, the hotel's website states the following: "Now, are we claiming that staying in this room will bring out your muse and you'll write the greatest novel of our times? No." What do I say, though? Believe it! I'd opt for proclaiming that Hemingway is *still* there. He's in the walls, in the halls, at that desk where he started plotting out *A Farewell to Arms*, and at that window pondering his next sentence.

Two people who often live in nice hotels for lengthy periods are John Travolta and his wife, Kelly Preston. One of the hotels they reside in is the Pink Beach Club in Bermuda. Travolta echoes what many actors have told me about choosing to live in hotels: "Because I've spent so much time living in hotels I've developed a real affinity for them. Once you find a good hotel, it becomes like a good restaurant or a good beach or something. It's a place you just want to either keep staying in or keep coming back to." And that becomes the challenge for any hotelier trying to establish a new hotel that won't just draw people in but will make them want to return to again and again.

One of the most decadent of the modern hotels I've spent time in has to be the Delano in Miami. High-flying hotelier Ian Schrager opened the Delano in the mid-1990s when South Beach was trying to become the new epicentre of cool in North

America. The Delano has a stark white art deco exterior and a dark wood and white lobby that is minimalist and made mysterious with tall, gauzy curtains that gently sway in the constant breeze. As for the suites in the hotel, they are white, white, and white! The first time I stayed in the Delano I felt I was in a psychiatric ward! The television was white, the walls were white, and the radio and telephone were white. The rear of the hotel features a pool that's more than somewhere to swim. It's like a wet nightclub — music is actually pumped in under the water, and there are a number of tables in the shallow end that allow you to lounge with a drink while partially immersed. Very quickly the Delano, which Schrager named after U.S. President Franklin Delano Roosevelt, became a hangout for supermodels and Madonna. It also became notorious for nude pool parties that lasted from midnight until 8:00 a.m.

My first experience at the Delano occurred in late October 1996 when I did interviews with the cast and crew of the film *Romeo + Juliet*, directed by Baz Luhrmann, the Australian artist/filmmaker. Luhrmann had originally intended to shoot in South Beach to give his movie a pastel art deco vibe, but cost and a change of thought had prompted him to shift the location to the cheaper and far more chaotic Mexico City.

On my way to Miami and the Delano, I picked up a paperback that contained Luhrmann's screenplay (with Craig Pearce) and the William Shakespeare play it was based on under the same cover. I read both with great interest in my suite in the Delano before heading out to see the film at a nearby Miami cinema. The next day I went to meet Luhrmann in his poolside suite. I found him to be a smart, engaging guy who was quite talkative but not pretentious in any way. He just loved to talk about his work, ideas, and inspirations. I shocked him when I said I thought the reverence surrounding all things Shakespeare was a bit misguided because the Bard in his day was someone who pumped out populist plays about politics, sex, violence, betrayal, and love for an audience of drunk punters who wanted to be entertained, not enlightened.

Luhrmann reached over and grasped my hand. "Thank you, mate. Thank you. I think the same way, but no one else wants to say that because it's just assumed you should like and admire and revere Shakespeare without putting any thought into it at all."

I went on to tell Luhrmann that I'd read his screenplay in my suite before meeting him. He asked me where I'd gotten a copy of the screenplay. I told him I'd bought it in a Toronto bookstore before coming to Miami. Luhrmann was dumbfounded. He wasn't aware that it had been published! He was quite upset about that and asked if we could stop the TV interview and go up to my suite to look at the book. I was a bit surprised but told him why not. We took off our microphones and walked up to my suite where I handed over the book.

Luhrmann seemed incensed. "It looks like a penny dreadful! Can I borrow this? I want to get to the bottom of why I'm holding this published edition of my work without being told it was being published."

I told him that was fine with me.

Later, in various suites in the Delano, I discussed *Romeo + Juliet* and life in general with Leonardo DiCaprio, Claire Danes, and the very engaging actor Harold Perrineau (Michael Dawson in *Lost* and Link in the *Matrix* films). During my conversation with Perrineau, we compared martial arts notes. He was a Chinese kung fu practitioner, and I mentioned to him that I'd studied Okinawan shorin-ryu karate. After the interview, Perrineau said he'd love to have a drink and talk martial arts later on if I was around. I said that would be cool, and we agreed to meet by the pool at 9:00 p.m.

That night we sat at one of the in-pool tables. As we chatted about various martial arts techniques, styles, and philosophies, micro-bikini-clad girls and their 70-year-old boyfriends frolicked in the water. Booze flowed everywhere, and there was lots of female giggling. After Perrineau and I had a couple of drinks, we shook hands and he headed off to a party while I went back to my suite. It was another dazzling evening of hotel surrealism, like a private party where everyone was welcome and no one was judged.

Ultimately, that's the main thing hotel living offers a guest: freedom without judgment. When you live in a hotel, for no matter how long, you behave at your own discretion, and as long as you don't bother your fellow guests, no one will interfere or cast a judgmental glance. If you annoy another guest, a good hotel staff won't try to blame one party over another. They will simply attempt to smooth the situation over so that everyone is happy again.

During all my time at the Royal York, I've only been complained about once, and it was minor. But in hotels seemingly trivial incidents can escalate into major problems if they aren't immediately and very diplomatically handled. One night after a long day of doing radio interviews on the phone promoting the book I did on Britney Spears, I poured some cognac and relaxed in bed with an old movie. The next thing I knew I was awakened by the phone ringing at almost three in the morning. I was disoriented for a moment because the TV was blaring a war movie and the lights were still on. When I answered the phone, I discovered it was the front desk asking me to turn down the television because it was disturbing the neighbouring guests. I quickly said I was sorry and that I'd fallen asleep with the TV on. Then I switched it off right away. I thought about running next door and personally apologizing to my neighbours but realized that would likely compound the situation.

One of the most dazzling of the modern hotels I've spent time in is the Four Seasons on 57th Street between Madison and Park Avenues, probably the finest location in all of New York for a hotel. It is ultra-sleek and modern, and at 52 storeys is the tallest hotel in New York and the third tallest in North America.

My first experience of the New York Four Seasons happened when I interviewed Kenneth Branagh, Robert De Niro, and Tom Hulce, an actor I'd always wanted to meet. Hulce played Mozart in the film version of *Amadeus*. Apart from the stunning interior design of the hotel by the architect I.M. Pei, the beautiful views of the city from its windows, the hydraulically opened drapes accessed from buttons in bedside tables, and the luxurious bathrooms Nero himself would have found comfortable, the thing I'll never forget is what happened when I first checked in. After I was given my key, I turned toward the bank of elevators and the desk person asked, or I thought he asked, "Will you be taking a bath, sir?"

I stepped back and said, "I'm sorry. Could you repeat that? I don't think I heard you correctly."

He then repeated his question word for word.

I chuckled, having never been asked such a question before upon checking into a hotel. "Perhaps I will," I said, "but may I know the intent of your question, sir?"

He smiled and explained that the water came out of the bathtub faucet with an unusual intensity, filling the tub in a few minutes. In the past, guests had turned on the faucets, then had made phone calls or watched TV without realizing how quickly the water was flowing, causing a number of floods. I nodded and thanked him for the advice but confirmed what he'd said as soon as I got into my suite. And, yes, the water did blast out of the ornate faucet as if it were geysering from a fire hose.

Security is something everyone I've ever spoken to or researched says is one of the big pluses when choosing to live in a hotel. I talked to John Travolta and Kelly Preston in early 2010 for a magazine profile about their decision to live a good portion of the year in Bermuda's Pink Beach Club Hotel. They told me that security was a big reason for their selecting that particular hotel, not to mention the 1,800 feet of oceanfront and two heavenly pink sand beaches. "When you're in a private residence," Travolta said, "you have to be conscious about security. You have to arrange it and maintain it and be aware of it. Here [the Pink Beach Club] good security is provided, so you can enjoy the seclusion of the place, and the privacy, without worrying about being safe, because that's provided for you."

Preston added that she loves living in hotels because of the communal spirit. "There's a feeling of being taken care of in hotels that's very comforting. If you want absolute privacy, that's what you can have, but anything you need or want can be arranged for you at a moment's notice. That's a wonderfully relaxing feeling, and because of how this hotel [the Pink Beach Club] is laid out, you can be secluded and social at the same time, in the same place."

Perhaps one of the stranger stories concerning a famous hotel resident and security is that of actor and bodybuilder Arnold Schwarzenegger, who won the governorship of California in 2003. Unlike a lot of states, California has no governor's mansion, so after his election, rather than seek out a private residence, Schwarzenegger moved into a spacious suite in the Hyatt Regency in the state capital of Sacramento. I called an aide to Governor Schwarzenegger to ask him a few questions about the arrangement. "I would imagine that having the governor living in a hotel, especially a large one catering to events and conventions," I said, "would pose any number of security problems. Have you found that to be the case?"

"You know," the aide responded, "we found that the opposite was true. The hotel has its own security apparatus in place that serves all guests already, so we had the advantage of having built-in security on top of the security detail provided to the governor by the state, something we wouldn't have had obviously if the governor had decided to live in a private residence."

I asked the aide about Schwarzenegger's decision to live in a hotel.

"Are you asking me about the decision for him to reside in that particular hotel? That I'm not sure of."

I told him I wasn't asking about any specific hotel, but merely the decision itself. Was it Schwarzenegger who suggested it?

"It was a decision Governor Schwarzenegger made himself shortly after winning the election," the aide said. "The governor has a beautiful home in Southern California [he has an 11,000-square-foot Brentwood mansion as well as large homes in Hyannis Port, Massachusetts, and Sun Valley, Idaho], and since his time in Sacramento is limited to his term as governor of California, he decided this would just be easier than finding a house, buying it, then selling it again once his time in Sacramento came to a close."

I suggested to the aide that because of Schwarzenegger's time in the movies he was used to living in hotels for long periods while on location, so he was already comfortable in them.

"I never thought of that," the aide said, "but that would make the decision make even more sense."

Finally, I asked the aide what Schwarzenegger's life was like in the Hyatt Regency Sacramento.

"Well, obviously he's pretty busy doing the business of California, but he does use the fitness facilities when he can. He's still a dedicated fitness enthusiast."

I asked the aide if the fitness area or pool had to be cleared and secured when Schwarzenegger used them.

"Oh, no, Governor Schwarzenegger loves to be around average people. I remember once he was in the gym and an older lady hotel guest asked him if he had some tips about the best kind of training for her to stay in shape. She was half joking, but Governor Schwarzenegger made a point of asking her questions about her health, then gave her some suggestions on what she should and shouldn't be doing."

When I spent some time at a hotel development in the Dominican Republic called Cap Cana doing a story on it, I had one of my oddest experiences concerning security. The development includes hotels, restaurants, a subdivision with houses, condos, a marina, a school, and a hospital. The area I was in was a resort that afforded each guest with his or her own private villa either backing onto a gorgeous beach on one side or a golf course on the other.

What was remarkable about these villas was that the living room, the dining room, and the kitchen were all open-air. There were no walls, just a few columns and a large thatched roof. The feeling you got standing in your living room with warm breezes caressing you and outdoor tropical sounds tickling your ears was astounding. The bedrooms and bathrooms were in separate little bungalows that did have doors and locks, of course, but the living area was shared with nature.

If you stay in one of the villas at the Dominican Republic's Cap Cana resort, you might well have someone like singer/actress Jennifer Lopez as a neighbour.

The villa opposite mine (I was sharing with ace *Toronto Star* travel writer Jim Byers) was occupied by Jennifer Lopez and her husband, Marc Anthony. This being the Dominican Republic, you would think such a resort would be crawling with security, especially given the open-air nature of the living spaces. And, in fact, the place *was* crawling with security. But the wonderful part was that you never spotted the security people, at least you didn't think you saw them. Certainly, uniformed security people were where you'd expect to find them, but there were also security types dressed as golfers, swimmers, and tourists. Cap Cana was the only hotel I've ever been in where you weren't issued a room key because you didn't need one. The only time you locked your bedroom door was when you were in the bedroom. That's how confident management was with its security standards. I never felt anything but completely relaxed and safe during my entire time at Cap Cana.

Hotels touch different people in different ways, of course. Many people would much rather sleep on the floor of a friend's place when visiting a city than stay in a hotel. Others find hotels today to be cold and corporate, feeling that they don't really matter to the hotel as people, that they're simply dollar signs for the ravenous accounting department to gobble up and add to the ledger. To some degree that's true out of pure necessity, especially in the past few years, but good hotels know they have to look beyond that if they're ever to have any kind of leg up on the competition. And while the general population can feel that living in a hotel for an extended period can be a lonely and cold existence, actors and musicians understand that the very isolation that might unnerve most people is nothing short of inspiring for them. Actor Matthew McConaughey once responded to a question I asked him about choosing to live in an RV rather than a house. "Yeah," he said, "I do like to be out there roughing it, exploring, seeing the country up close. But I'll tell you, brother, as much as I dig that, I still love my Four Seasons."

As I've said previously, of all the hotels I've been in and discussed with others, my favourite is still Toronto's Royal York. When sifting through the stories about other grand hotels, and some not so grand, when hearing from other people why they prefer hotel life, I can't stop thinking that perhaps I didn't choose the Royal York, after all. Maybe it picked me.

BOOK TWO

SOME KIND
OF
EPIC GRANDEUR

I REMEMBER THE FIRST TIME I WALKED into the Royal York Hotel. I might have been in the building before this memory, but it is ingrained as the first occasion the hotel's epic grandeur had a real impact on me. I was quite young, no more than ten years old, and I was going on a train trip with my father to Montreal and we were leaving from Union Station. We were on our way to Central Station in Montreal to stay in the Queen Elizabeth Hotel. I recall walking through the Royal York's lobby, which was almost exactly as it is today, and I remember not being able to do anything except gaze up at the chandeliers, at the mezzanine railings and flags, at the immensity of it all.

My father and I sat in front of the reception desk for a while until it was time to catch our train. I watched people coming and going, many smiling or laughing. Groups of well-dressed guests gathered before attending weddings or dinners. I'd never seen any place like this, never been somewhere that was so cavernous, never felt overwhelmed by something so splendid and warmly enveloping at the same time. Even now that first memory has a strange quality that makes me ask: "Did I live that, or did I just dream it?"

So just how did the "palace" of my early memories begin? Actually, its establishment dates indirectly back to 1907 when two San Francisco dreamers, Tessie and Virginia Fair, set their imaginations to building the Fairmont, the finest hotel in the world. Their determination was challenged, but their resolve certainly wasn't, when they were forced to delay the opening of their hotel by more than a year after the 1906 earthquake that flattened San Francisco. But they did open it, and the rest is hotel history.

However, the Royal York's origins lie even farther in the past than 1907. On July 30, 1793, the schooner *Mississauga*, carrying Lieutenant Governor John Graves Simcoe and his wife, Elizabeth, sailed into the harbour of what eventually became first York, then Toronto, the future capital of Upper Canada.

Simcoe was a smart strategist and was thinking ahead about how to best defend the colony's territory against the United States and France, especially since Britain was at war with the latter and the former was a French ally. He believed time was of the essence, and after studying maps and charts decided the harbour he was now anchored in was an excellent location for a naval arsenal. Simcoe named the new town York to honour the Duke of York, King George III's second eldest son and a notable military commander. The newly minted lieutenant governor brought in surveyors who designed a ten-square-block grid for his new municipality, but it wasn't until 1801 that John Jordan's York Hotel, the first of its kind, was erected on the eastern side of town where currently the Toronto Sun Building is situated. Although York was designated the capital of Upper Canada in 1796, that wasn't saying much, since the colony only possessed about 25,000 souls and York itself boasted a mere 600. Most of the early citizens of York were soldiers and government officials.

In 1843 Thomas Dick, a navy captain, opened Ontario Terrace, which consisted of four interconnected commercial buildings on Front Street. Ten years after Dick started Ontario Terrace, the complex was renovated and the four structures were consolidated and rechristened Sword's Hotel. Upper Canada grew rapidly, and in 1841 Britain merged it and Lower Canada (renamed Canada East, now Quebec) into the United Province of Canada. York, rechristened Toronto in 1834, was stripped of its status as capital of Upper Canada (renamed Canada West, now Ontario) when Kingston became the seat of government for the amalgamated colony. During the 26-year history of the United Province of Canada (1841–1867), the capital shifted frequently, alternating between Montreal, Toronto, Quebec City, and finally Ottawa. Sword's Hotel, meanwhile, was sold and its name was changed to Revere House.

As Toronto mushroomed and its population diversified, the need for a much bigger hotel was answered in 1862 when Revere House was renamed the Queen's Hotel and two new additions were constructed, one on either end, transforming the Queen's into a luxury hostelry. That first incarnation had one of the finest restaurants in Canada West, with 210 bedchambers and 70 private parlours. The hotel boasted that it could comfortably accommodate 400 guests and was the first such establishment in the colony. It was also the first hotel in Canada to offer running water to guests as well as a hot air furnace and a telephone for guest use in the lobby. Two large, beautifully maintained gardens were eventually added to further enhance comfort and relaxation for guests.

The Queen's Hotel was part of a magnificent era of palatial North American hotels, places that were created not just as inns with bedrooms for weary travellers to sleep in but as luxurious, extravagant establishments where important people could meet, relax, and enjoy the finest of everything. Such grand hotels were usually built by railway barons in both Britain and North America. In 1839 the opulent Royal Western Hotel opened its doors in Bristol, England, while the Adelaide and Victoria Hotels commenced business in London. In Canada the first truly grand hotel was Montreal's Windsor Hotel, which started life in 1878.

The Montreal-based Canadian Pacific Railway devised ambitious plans for opening lavish hotels along its coast-to-coast rail line, including ones in Banff, Alberta (Banff Springs), and Quebec City (Château Frontenac). When Montreal's Mount Royal Hotel was opened in 1923, it gave Canadian Pacific boss Edward Wentworth Beatty a bold idea: he commissioned the firm responsible for the Mount Royal to design and erect the poshest hotel not just in the CPR chain but in the British Empire. Beatty began talks with the architectural firm of Ross & Macdonald, which was also involved with Hugh Jones and John Lyle in the construction of Toronto's Union Station, a gigantic project that was officially opened in 1927.

Beatty had his sights set on the Queen's Hotel. The people of Toronto naturally assumed Canadian Pacific would buy the Queen's and renovate it into something even more magnificent than it was, but Beatty's vision was more extravagant than that. His plan was to buy the Queen's Hotel, raze it completely, and erect an entirely new, much more sumptuous hotel. Torontonians were quite upset with Beatty and the CPR, since the Queen's Hotel had become a comfortable landmark, a place of gathering, so the idea that this railway baron was just going to stroll in and tear it down caused some irate reactions.

In the 1920s life was changing rapidly. The idea of acquiring wealth was now thought of as something anyone resourceful and ingenious enough could attain rather than merely for people born to the manor. The development of the automobile as an accepted, accessible, and commonplace mode of transportation transformed travel and allowed people to journey from their own regions more than ever before. Meanwhile, world economies were expanding and flourishing.

For Beatty, building his hotel directly across the street from the brand-new Union Station made perfect sense. As soon as the Queen's Hotel was demolished in 1927, Ross & Macdonald and Sproatt & Rolph, the two architectural firms Beatty enlisted for his ambitious project, along with the contractor Anglia Novercross, went to work to make the CPR boss's dream

This early poster, circa 1928, depicts the Royal York Hotel before it was actually opened the next year.

become a reality. As the Royal York rose, journalists sang its praises, with one reporter writing that Beatty was "building a magnificent mountain to tower over a city and a lake."

The Art Deco style of the Royal York provides a sharp contrast to the long, low, colonnaded Beaux Art Union Station. The hotel is a towering 28 storeys of steel frame encased in Indiana limestone rising dramatically in ornate steps to a steeply pitched copper château roof. Personally speaking, my favourite architectural details of the Royal York are the griffins and gargoyles that loom over its various corners and peaks. The initial image I saw the first morning I woke up in the Royal York after moving in was the griffin I spied from my bed. Not a day has gone by that I haven't looked at that mighty creature at least once.

The griffin is a mythological creature with the body of a lion and the head and wings of an eagle. The earliest depictions of griffins are the frescoes in the throne room of the Bronze Age Palace of Knossos on Crete. The beast continued being a preferred decorative theme in Archaic and Classical Greek art. In Central Asia the griffin appears about 1,000 years after Bronze Age Crete in the fifth and fourth century B.C., probably originating from the Achaemenid Persian Empire. The Achaemenids considered the griffin "a protector from evil, witchcraft, and secret slander."

It makes good sense to me why griffins were chosen to watch over the Royal York. Gargoyles, on the other hand, have a more practical architectural purpose in that they are usually placed in areas on a roof that require drainage. An elongated, fantastical stone animal has a spout cut in it to convey water from the roof and away from the side of a building because running water erodes the mortar between stone blocks. This kind of use for the gargoyle dates back to ancient Egypt, even though the more contemporary application is strictly decorative. You can see the Royal York's gargoyles and griffins from the street and from many of the suite windows in the hotel, but if you manage to see them up close from the high rooftops of the hotel, it is then that they assume their true power.

The truly interesting aspect of the Royal York's design, and one feature that a person isn't generally conscious of until it is pointed out, is the fact that the ground floor and the floor below it, the A Floor, are laid out like a commercial square in a town. The main part of the lobby and the front desk area are the town square, with long corridors featuring restaurants, barbershops, and cafés extending out from it. Originally, there was also a marble-and-terrazzo tunnel linking the lower A Floor of the hotel with Union Station so that guests had the convenience of getting to their train without leaving the building. This passageway is now part of the PATH network of tunnels that spreads underground throughout downtown Toronto.

Where the guest rooms themselves were concerned, once again serious thought was put into the hotel's layout. The main

This stone griffin looks down on Toronto from the north exterior wall of the Royal York.

(Courtesy Fairmont Hotels & Resorts)

11 floors of guest rooms were designed in an H configuration so that virtually every room in the hotel received natural light during the day.

The building of the Royal York started in 1927 and was completed two years later, with the doors opening on June 11, 1929, for what became one of the biggest social gatherings in Toronto's history, complete with Viscount Willingdon, governor general of Canada, in attendance with 1,430 of the city's top business leaders. Later that same evening a soiree was staged for the general public at $10 per person, and the attendees were told what a special treat it was to be there, since the hotel wouldn't receive guests officially until the next day.

The first six months in the long history of the Royal York were furiously energetic. News releases raved about the 1,945 beds, the ten tons of ice cubes used each day, the 36,000 gallons of hot water consumed every hour, and the fact that the roof garden lounge had the highest dance floor and dining lounge in the British Empire. The Horace Walker Library, one of the most beautiful rooms in the entire hotel, was stocked with more than 12,000 books selected by Dr. George Locke, Toronto's chief librarian of the day. The hotel also boasted such added unique touches as a large children's playroom, a 12-bed hospital with a doctor and nurse standing by at all times, and a convention area, with a huge pipe organ, built to accommodate as many as 4,000 people. Because the operation of such a city within a city was so complex, the top four floors of the hotel were devoted to motors and cables to drive the elevators, water tanks, ventilation equipment, and a workshop for the other workers and craftsman on hand such as silversmiths. Rather than use coal as the energy source, the Royal York wisely chose live steam sent in under high pressure via pipes from a nearby plant called Terminal Company.

The Royal York cost just over $16 million to complete, a miniscule amount by today's standards, but a truly impressive sum in those days. The Royal Architectural Institute of Canada awarded the Royal York its gold medal in 1930 and described the building in a proclamation accompanying the award:

> This building can, without question, be considered one of the most important structures erected in Canada during recent years. It is to the credit of architects, Messrs. Ross and Macdonald, of Montreal, with whom were associated Messrs. Sproatt and Rolph, of Toronto, that they have not only succeeded in designing a modern and complete hotel for that most enterprising of Canadian corporations — the Canadian Pacific Railway — but they have also provided the city of Toronto with a monument that its citizens may well be proud of.

One early guest reported checking into the hotel for his honeymoon just after the opening in July 1929, as my parents did for their honeymoon 35 years later almost to the day. "I walked up to the desk with my new bride and asked for a deluxe room," said the man. "It cost $5 at that time. I had my marriage licence in my pocket and was ready to produce it if they asked me about checking into the hotel with a pretty young girl. I was surprised when the desk clerk didn't even ask me for it." After an enjoyable honeymoon, this man and his wife were still married to each other 60 years later. So to celebrate that milestone they returned to the Royal York. "The room we had way back then was occupied," said the man, "but when the folks at the hotel heard my story, they gave us a great big room and put flowers and champagne in it. It was wonderful."

Winston Churchill was one of the first big-name dignitaries to speak at the Royal York. Before Churchill appeared at the Royal York's Empire Club on August 16, 1929, a huge crowd gathered outside the hotel, hoping to catch a glimpse of him. The hotel then decided to set up a temporary loudspeaker system so that those outside could hear the British politician's speech.

Then, as now, the Royal York had the biggest hotel kitchen in the country (100 chefs still work in it), and one floor below the enormous kitchen is the equally impressive laundry room. The giant clothes dryer takes care of enough laundry in one load to hang dry on more than 12 miles of clothesline.

Amid all the hoopla and hype the Royal York rightly enjoyed, the fame of the place meant it was a lightning rod for more nefarious things such as something that began on August 14, 1934. Multimillionaire beer magnate John Sackville Labatt began his day at a rented summer home in Sarnia, Ontario, with the intention of driving to his brewery's headquarters in London, Ontario, for a meeting. After leaving the house, Labatt noticed that a car was following him. The car then passed his, but when Labatt rounded a bend, he was startled to see the car dead ahead and blocking the road.

Three gun-toting hoods pulled Labatt from his car and forced him to write a letter to his brother, Hugh, saying that he was in the custody of armed gunmen who would kill him if a ransom of $150,000 in cash wasn't paid (which, in today's dollars, is about $2.5 million). The letter instructed Hugh to head immediately to the Royal York Hotel, check in, and await further instructions. One of the kidnappers signed the letter "Three-Finger Abe."

The letter was delivered as Labatt was taken to a secluded cottage in Bracebridge, Ontario. The plan was to have Hugh wrangle together the cash, then either get someone to meet him at the Library Bar in the Royal York for the switch or have Hugh take the money to a secluded spot and dump it there. For some reason Hugh immediately informed the press about the kidnapping, but did as instructed and went to the Royal York to check in and wait. The next day the *Toronto Star*'s headline read: WHAT HAS THREE-FINGER ABE DONE WITH JOHN LABATT?

The hoods kept Labatt blindfolded and chained to a bed in the rural cottage for a couple of days to allow Hugh time to gather the cash, then Hugh was instructed to take the money and dump it over a bridge about ten miles north of the Royal York. The kidnappers were getting more spooked by the media attention by the minute. What Three-Finger Abe and his confederates thought would be a simple grab for cash had turned into a countrywide *cause célèbre*, and they were sure that Hugh had provided the police with virtually every detail of Abe's instructions, which meant they could be ambushed by the cops at any moment during the switch.

After the kidnappers brought Labatt into town to release him for the money, they panicked and abandoned the scheme altogether. Labatt had about $100 in cash on him, so they seized that, gave the brewing magnate a dollar for cab fare, and released him pretty much unharmed halfway between where they said they wanted the ransom delivered and the Royal York. Labatt jumped into the first taxi that passed and asked to be dropped off at the Royal York. When he arrived at the hotel, he walked in through the front door and into the lobby. Police and newspaper men were everywhere, but Labatt didn't know who they were or why they were there, and they didn't recognize him. Labatt made his way through the crowd and the din to the reception desk where he told the man there that his brother was staying in the hotel. At this point one of the reporters recognized Labatt, and "hysterical bedlam," as one journalist later wrote, broke out in the lobby.

There are two interesting footnotes to the story: John Labatt was so traumatized by the affair that he became a virtual recluse until his death in 1952, and two of the hoods were caught immediately, but the third escaped to the United States (where he was later murdered by another criminal a few years later. The two who were captured were given 12- to 15-year prison sentences. A third man was arrested for the crime, someone Labatt clearly and positively identified as the third fellow involved in his kidnapping, but the man turned out to be completely innocent. He, too, was sentenced to a 12- to 15-year prison stretch. However, the man maintained his innocence, and 13 months later he was freed when it was proven he couldn't have been the third kidnapper. He sued Labatt, and the beer tycoon settled by giving him $5,500 for his trouble and time.

(Courtesy Fairmont Hotels & Resorts)

Right from the beginning the Royal York was a nexus for Toronto's busy urban life, as this photograph from the 1930s attests.

Many years later another incident happened that illustrates the wildly divergent group of people that can be found under the Royal York's roof at any time. This strange event unfolded on March 9, 1987, during a convention in the hotel that brought together miners and prospectors from around the world. One local man attending the convention was Timmins's André Bissonette, who was the owner, with his wife, of a circus called Magic World. Bissonette's wife and two young sons were then in Venezuela touring with the circus. On the evening in question, Bissonette was having a heated conversation with Guy-Maurice Lamarche, another conventioneer who owned Cleyo Resources, a small mining exploration company. The discussion/argument between the two grew angrier and angrier on the C Floor (Convention Floor) until finally Bissonette pulled out a .38 calibre handgun, aimed it point-blank at Lamarche's chest, and fired twice.

Bissonette ran clumsily down the up escalator as Lamarche slumped to the floor dead. The shooter rushed through the lobby and out onto York Street where he quickly flagged the first taxi he saw. The taxi headed north but got less than two blocks when it was boxed in by police cars, sirens wailing. Police officers surrounded the cab. Bissonette still had the gun but didn't fire again and was disarmed quickly, taken into custody, and charged with first-degree murder. One of the conventioneers who witnessed the event said at the time: "The mining business can be tough."

The above incident followed an even deadlier one in the Royal York that occurred 12 years earlier, the savagery of which is hard even to fathom, given the calming and relaxing nature of the hotel. It happened on September 18, 1975. A guest checked into the hotel using a credit card that was later determined to have been stolen in the United States. The assistant credit manager, Lyanage Pryel De Silva, a recent immigrant from Sri

Lanka, was sent to the man's room to investigate. Because this was a bit more serious than a routine question being asked, De Silva, who was only 22 at the time, was accompanied by Roger Saunders, a Canadian Pacific security officer, and Gary Silliker, a Toronto police officer. Silliker was asked to assist in case the guest was a wanted criminal in the United States and because the man was using stolen property.

The group went up to the eighth floor and knocked on the guest's door. The guest opened the door without incident and let them in. He then pulled out a gun and aimed it at his visitors. Saunders darted into the bathroom of the suite where he was shot in the stomach. The gunman then aimed the weapon at the face of Constable Silliker, who raised his arms to shield his head and was struck by a bullet in the back of the shoulder. The terrified De Silva bolted out of the suite and down the hallway. When he realized he was running the wrong way, he reversed direction, a decision that cost him his life.

The gunman darted into the hallway and fired at the fleeing De Silva several times. The Royal York employee was hit first in the leg, then in the head. The murderer, later identified as Roy Allen Embry of Louisville, Kentucky, was able to get to the lobby, exit the hotel, and flee in a car bearing Kentucky plates. Toronto police were tipped that the fugitive was in Niagara Falls, so they quickly travelled there to nab him, but by the time they arrived, Embry had slipped back into the United States at the border crossing. Warrants for the gunman's arrest on one count of murder and two counts of attempted murder were issued. Later Embry turned up in Denver, Colorado, where he shot and killed a policeman and wounded another officer trying to apprehend him on the Canadian warrant and other warrants for crimes committed in Kentucky. Embry was wounded in the gunfight but lived.

Of course, not all dust-ups in the Royal York have been as violent and horrific as the Embry affair. In 1961 Irish raconteur and playwright Brendan Behan was staying in the Royal York while performing down the street at the O'Keefe Centre (now the Sony Centre). After drinking non-stop on the day his show was to open, Behan staggered onto the stage roaring drunk. He barely made it through the evening, then tottered back to the Royal York to look for something more to drink. By this time it was well past the time liquor could legally be served publicly, so Behan was denied. The playwright then roamed the lobby, halls, and mezzanine, yelling about how ridiculous Ontario liquor laws were and how he couldn't understand them. Eventually, he was confronted by a hotel detective who tried to reason with him. Behan, though, decided there was only one way to settle their differences — boxing. The two traded punches, but the house detective came out on the short end. Behan continued his drunken protest until Toronto police arrived. The playwright was given the choice of spending the night in the comfort of his Royal York suite or sleeping the night off in the Don Jail. Wisely, Behan picked the former.

One of the things the Royal York established early on and maintains to this day is the idea that it is the perfect place for business meetings and commemorative dinners. One of the most interesting special dinners held at the Royal York occurred on April 15, 1939. That date is significant because it was the anniversary of the sinking of the *Titanic*, and the guests at this particular supper were Elizabeth Mellinger, Madeleine Mellinger Mann, Emma Bliss, and Samuel Collins, four survivors of the disaster who got together at the Royal York to mark their survival and memorialize the tragedy.

Thousands of weddings, parties, and celebrations have been held at the Royal York over the years. Most are notable only to those in attendance, but there have been occasions when celebrations got out of hand. One such affair happened on the night of April, 13, 1940. The National Hockey League's New York Rangers had just beaten the Toronto Maple Leafs with an overtime goal in game six to win the Stanley Cup. The team hastily booked one of the party rooms in the Royal York, since it was the hotel the team was staying in. They reserved a small room for a celebration involving the players, team executives, coaching staff, and any family or friends on hand — all told about 35 people.

In a larger room nearby a bigger party was going on, with lots of dancing and drinking and a crowd of hundreds. When a member of the larger party caught a glimpse of the Stanley Cup being brought into the adjoining room, word spread like wildfire. Soon the little gathering of players, coaches, and friends was overrun by hundreds of party crashers eager for a glimpse of the Stanley Cup and the players who had won it. What started as a small get-together turned into a raucous celebration in the hometown of the team the Rangers had trounced to win the championship!

A few years later the lobby of the Royal York became the scene of another weird sporting celebration, this time in the form of a stampede. Fans of the Canadian Football League's Calgary Stampeders were dressed in western regalia and having a drunken party on the streets of Toronto when some of them decided it would make a newsworthy splash if they rode their horses into the Royal York. One group held the doors open while the horsemen galloped into the lobby, whooping and hollering.

And that wasn't the last Grey Cup drama to visit the Royal York. Say what you will about docile Canadians, but when a sports celebration is at hand, Canadian fans can tear it up with the best of them. On one occasion, in 1956, the then manager of the Royal York was so anxious about what might happen after the Grey Cup championship game between the Edmonton Eskimos and the Montreal Alouettes that he ordered all the furniture removed from the lobby and the mezzanine two full days before the game was to be played on Saturday.

Another Canadian football story happened in the Royal York on November 27, 1965. Newly fired Montreal Alouettes coach Jim Trimble met with Ian MacDonald, a reporter from the now-defunct *Montreal Star*, to do an interview in the Royal York where they were both staying. The conversation got heated and led to Trimble throwing a few punches at MacDonald. The skirmish was quickly put aside, and the two took their conversation outdoors in the cool November air to talk while walking down to the waterfront. By the time the pair got there, the discussion had devolved into more punches being thrown by Trimble. Since both were staying in the Royal York, they headed back there separately. Upon coming together in the lobby, Trimble again went after the sportswriter physically. As soon as Trimble was pulled off MacDonald and the two went to their respective rooms, the journalist reported the assault to the police and to the CFL. Trimble later made a public apology to MacDonald.

After the 1970 Grey Cup final, rowdy fans took over the Royal York and transformed it into a giant drunk. When hotel security and staff felt they were losing control, the police were called in. As soon as the police arrived, they gently tried to diffuse the situation so that a happy celebration wouldn't turn into a riot. The police were greeted by drunks passed out everywhere. Those who weren't unconscious were swinging from the railings on the mezzanine. The police made over 200 arrests that November evening. Many were released shortly after but were detained to prevent them from doing further damage to the Royal York, while others were held for a day or two longer to think over the kind of choices they would make the next time they wanted to celebrate.

One of the things the rowdy 1970 crowd was celebrating might have been the fact there was a Grey Cup at all. The previous December the Grey Cup was heisted by a couple of Toronto bozos from its home in Ottawa. The pair demanded a large ransom for the trophy, but got nowhere since they were asking for a sum many times what the hardware was worth and it was cheaper for the CFL to make a new Grey Cup. Then Gordon Lennox, a Toronto police sergeant, got an anonymous tip, indicating that the Cup could be found in a locker in the Royal York and the key to that locker was taped under a telephone in a booth at the corner of Dundas and Parliament Streets. The police went to the phone booth and got the key, then went to the Royal York and retrieved the Cup. It was returned to the CFL a couple of days before the league was about to strike a new trophy.

The Royal York became part of another, more serious drama in September 1949. The *Noronic*, a Great Lakes cruise ship, was docked in Toronto's harbour on the other side of Union Station. The ship caught fire and the flames spread rapidly, causing the tragic loss of 118 passengers, with scores more injured. The management of the Royal York instantly threw open the hotel's doors so that the building could serve as an emergency field hospital to treat survivors.

To this day on the wall in the elegant Royal York mezzanine are two framed menus from the hotel restaurant circa 1929. Looking at these menus provides a fascinating glimpse at the way people ate back then. Take the breakfast menu, for example. One side records the larger 75-cent menu with such items as pork chops, Royal York sausages, chipped beef in cream, baked apples in cream, and stewed rhubarb. The leaner 50-cent menu includes stewed prunes with cream, stewed figs in cream, and sliced bananas in cream. The beverage offerings feature selections from a company called Adanac (Canada spelled backward): apple nectar, cream soda, ginger ale, ginger beer, and table water. Then, and this I find really funny, there are beverages from other companies: Canada Dry ginger ale, Cartell and Cochran ginger ale, Imperial Dry ginger ale, O'Keefe's dry ginger ale, Schweppes ginger ale, White Rock ginger ale, and Grand's ginger ale. Apparently, Canadians loved ginger ale in the late 1920s. They also liked something called Duncan's aperient water.

In 1930, a year after the menus showcasing all manner of items in cream and a plethora of ginger ales, Canadian Pacific Railway established its own radio station on the top floor of the Royal York. A full studio could accommodate bands playing live music and present talk shows and live dramas. Almost instantly the radio station gained a reputation as one of the finest in the country.

However, in the 1950s the Royal York briefly lost its title as the biggest hotel in the British Empire to the Queen Elizabeth Hotel in Montreal. So in 1957 (work completed in 1959) an addition was built onto the east end of the Royal York that added another 400 guest rooms and allowed the Royal York to regain its British Empire bragging rights. The east wing joins the main hotel by a linkage of the two significant cornerstones, one dated 1928, the other 1957. The design of the new east wing was awarded to a Montreal-based firm to tackle — Ross, Patterson, Townsend, & Fish, in association with Charles Dolphin of

Toronto. When the new wing opened officially on February 21, 1959, CPR boss N.R. Crump described the real reason for the enlargement. It wasn't to reclaim the title of largest hotel in the British Empire but was more in recognition of the fact that Toronto had become the convention capital of the nation and larger facilities were needed to meet new demands.

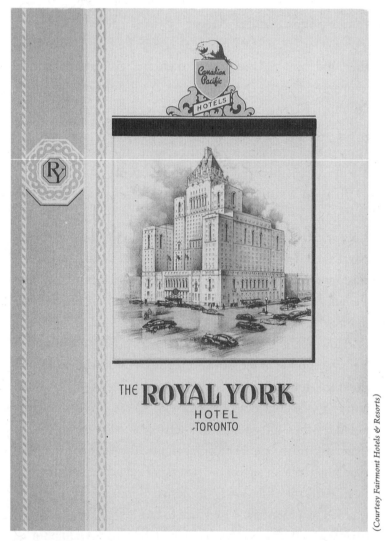

This Royal York menu cover dates back to 1952.

(Courtesy Fairmont Hotels & Resorts)

One of the additions was the Canadian Room, which replaced the old banquet hall. The Canadian Room boasted a seating capacity of 2,200 for meetings and 1,550 for banquets. It also had a hidden hydraulic system that could hoist trucks and other heavy exhibits onto the convention room floor. The Canadian Room featured a huge illuminated global projection relief map of Canada and a relief of the Canadian coat of arms carved from a slab of Canadian elm. The fabric of the walls incorporated elements of the Canadian coat of arms. The walls had backlit glass panels on which were etched the coats of arms of the Canadian provinces and territories. The doors were tempered plate glass incised with the Tudor rose, the maple leaf, and the fleur-de-lys. The ceiling of the Canadian Room was a startling addition to the overall design in that it was brightly coloured with undulating translucent aluminum panels and wide plaster ribs.

The Canadiana theme was carried over to the other meeting rooms of the new wing, as well. The interior designer responsible for the upgrades was Ernest Rex, and he brought in a group of Canadian artisans to decorate each of the meeting rooms in the hotel to highlight the role Canadian Pacific played in the development of Canada. The meeting space built to adjoin the Canadian Room was called the Ontario Room, the largest of the provincial rooms. It was decorated with 16 baseboard planter boxes whose inlaid fruitwood panels illustrated scenes from the history of Ontario. The Ontario Room had polished mother-of-pearl tile walls and four chandeliers that looked like handbaskets of trilliums, the official flower of the province. The chandeliers were suspended from a ceiling of gold-coloured aluminum.

While the two largest meeting rooms were part of the Convention Floor, the rest of the meeting rooms named after Canadian provinces were on the mezzanine level. They were

much smaller but were designed in keeping with the overall
provincial cultural theme. For example, the British Columbia
Room had wall panelling of British Columbia fir, eight totem
poles, carved wainscoting with Pacific Coast Native motifs, and
a hand-painted B.C. coat of arms in carved pine.

Today one of the most striking things about the Royal York's
lobby is the marble circular staircase that descends from the
main lobby to the lower A Floor and winds around an ornate
clock stand. Many people assume the staircase has been there
since the hotel's opening, but actually it wasn't added until
1973 when Royal York Revelation, a program to modernize the
hotel without diminishing its Old World charm and allure, was
put into effect under the direction of Webb, Zerafa, Menkes,
Housden, which was already busy designing the Royal Bank
Plaza rising next door. The architectural firm also enclosed the
marble pillars in the Royal York's lobby with wood panelling
and installed a number of wall lamps and another chandelier
and replaced all the rugs with carpeting.

That same year saw another visit to the Royal York by Queen
Elizabeth II and Prince Philip. In June 1973 the royal couple was
ensconced in the Royal Suite, otherwise known as suite 16-161.
The Royal Suite overlooks Toronto's waterfront, which today,
of course, means a view of glass-and-steel business and condo-
minium towers. A large fireplace dominates the living room of
the suite, and the walls are adorned with antique gold grasscloth
in 18th-century style. The two bedrooms on the other side of
the suite are self-contained and have their own bathrooms. In
the master bedroom there is an antique king-sized bed of carved
oak. When the queen is in town, she has specially designed

bedspreads. For the queen's 1973 visit the Royal York had three sets of specially designed china commissioned — an Aynsley, a Royal Doulton, and a Wedgewood, one for each meal Her Royal Highness ate during her stay.

The VIP suites (which include the Prime Minister's Suite and the Governor General's Suite) are furnished with an eye toward maintaining the original feel of the hotel. The dining rooms in these suites are done up in orange, rust, and pumpkin hues and have gold velvet curtains and enormous mahogany tables that seat 20.

During the 1980s, the ultra-luxurious Roof Garden Ballroom on the 19th floor, once a world-famous spot, was closed due to new fire safety regulations. While not used anymore for their original purpose, parts of the ballroom are now employed as office space and for public functions. Having explored the 19th floor, I can attest that the Royal Garden Ballroom is still magnificent.

The merger of Canadian Pacific Hotels & Resorts and Fairmont Hotels occurred in October 1999, resulting in the newly christened Fairmont Hotels and Resorts. Plans were immediately tabled to give the Royal York's lobby and mezzanine meeting rooms a further makeover. The refurbishment almost amounted dollar for dollar to the entire cost of building the hotel in the late 1920s. The restoration program expenditures totalled more than $12 million, with another $2.5 million spent to restore the Imperial Room, the Library Bar, and the connecting foyer. During these renovations, EPIC, the hotel's new restaurant, was built into the main lobby. In 2001 Deborah Lloyd Forrest, an American interior designer, was commissioned to design the Royal York's new marble mosaic tile floors.

~ ~ ~

A lot of people can't hear the name Royal York Hotel without immediately thinking of the Imperial Room, which from 1948 to 1972 was quite simply the hottest nightspot in Canada. After 1972 there was a valiant effort to maintain that status, but given changing audience tastes and the competition for entertainment dollars from so many other available sources, it was a lost cause. However, the Imperial Room remains, still grand and regal, still reverberating with the spirits, sounds, and excitement that took place here on a nightly basis for many decades.

Physically, the Imperial Room is an interesting space. You go through the lobby and up a few steps into the room, but the main floor and seating area are sunken a few steps. The stage isn't very high and takes up the north portion of the room. There is a main area where the circular tables are, and a behind-the-brass railing section where B-listers were once seated. Across the south wall is an elevated area with long booths and tables situated high enough so guests could look over the room with a clear view of the stage and the small hardwood dance floor in front. That south wall is where A-listers were seated. When Louis Janetta, the maître d', seated guests, they always glanced south toward the back wall to see the movers and shakers and stars in attendance.

During those glorious years at the Imperial Room, two men became the faces of the joint. The aforementioned Louis Janetta was known as a top Canadian impresario and one of the best maître d's anywhere. Every night he was the fellow who looked you over and took you to your table. Janetta was the man who told headliner Tony Bennett's manager he couldn't enter because of the strict dress code. Rules were rules, and at the Imperial Room Louis Janetta reigned supreme.

Janetta is a fascinating character, and his time at the Royal York encompassed much more than his years working in the

Imperial Room. In fact, he started at the Royal York as a busboy when he was only 14. "I told them I was 16, and they bought it," Janetta once said. He began a lifelong adventure that included everything from staring wide-eyed at heavyweight boxing champion Joe Louis as he cleared plates from the man's table, to rubbing elbows with a lot of raucous army and navy officers during the Second World War as they stopped by the Venetian Room (where EPIC is now) for breakfast and to share stories of the war.

It wasn't until 1963 that Janetta became the maître d' of the Imperial Room, which then had a staff of 85. He also oversaw the newly opened Black Knight Room (located where Piper's Gastro Pub is now), which was more of a jazzy supper club with a Harlem-style vibe. In fact, under Janetta's watch Shirlee May, a Harlem club jazz singer regular, played the Black Knight Room and had the distinction of being the first black performer to play there.

Many people believe that Janetta kicked Bob Dylan out of the Imperial Room in 1986 for not adhering to the dress code, but it was actually the Black Knight Room that Dylan wasn't allowed to enter because of his attire. Dylan was trying to get in to catch Tina Turner's act.

Janetta later told *National Post* reporter Karen Hawthorne: "For decades it [the Imperial Room] was one of the greatest dining rooms in all of North America — the chandeliers, the chateaubriand steak, the 12-piece big band for dinner and dancing, and of course my great friend, Tony Bennett, stopping by to do shows regularly." Patti Janetta, the maître d's daughter, actually got to perform on the Imperial Room stage twice, and when it came time for her to marry, where did she spend her wedding night? The Royal York, of course. Louis Janetta left the Royal York in 1990 after 50 years of service and high living.

The other big man at the Royal York was Moxie Whitney. From 1948 to 1972 you could hear the swinging sounds of the Moxie Whitney Orchestra every single night, with the exception of 1960–61. That year saw a long and contentious strike among the workers of the Royal York, and everything seemed to grind to a halt. In 1972 there was an equally touchy negotiation between Whitney and the Canadian Pacific brass, who still owned the Royal York then. Moxie wanted his long years of service reflected in his new contract, while Canadian Pacific believed big bands were a thing of the past and audiences wanted entertainment that was more relevant. Since both Moxie and Canadian Pacific had valid positions and were determined to stick to them, they decided by mutual arrangement to dissolve their professional association.

A new kind of promoter was brought into the Imperial Room to usher in a modern scene. His name was Gino Empry, and he was something of a legend himself. Empry was known for being Tony Bennett's manager for 12 years, and it was his idea to bring a Broadway-style show vibe or Las Vegas glitz to the Imperial Room to give younger audiences something they'd never seen there before.

Long after Empry left the Imperial Room, I interviewed him on *Daytime*, a talk show I once sub-hosted. My lifelong love affair with the Royal York was already in full bloom at the time, so naturally I peppered Empry with questions about the hotel. Empry was a distinctive-looking man, he dressed in a unique combination of glitz and cheese, and he spoke quickly and enthusiastically. "Remember, the Imperial Room was the biggest of the big," he told me. "I mean, every big swing act in the world played the Imperial Room, and not just played it, played the hell out of it. Many did some of their best shows in that room because the space and the crowd brought that out in them."

I asked Empry about some of those headliners who came before his years at the Imperial Room. "Are you kidding me?" he asked. "Who didn't play that room? Duke Ellington, Count Basie, Pearl Bailey, Woody Herman, Peggy Lee, Eartha Kitt, Marlene Dietrich, of course, and one of my favourite acts to watch there was Buddy Rich, the drummer. That guy would play the Imperial Room and beat the skins off his drums. He was exhausted, and the audience was exhausted, after he ended a set."

We then spoke about the transition between what the Imperial Room was in those swing days and what he was expected to do to change it while maintaining its status. "Well, you know, I saw something happening in show business, and I wanted to tap into it. The thing I was seeing was a lot of Canadian acts breaking out all over the place and having hit records and headlining shows in Vegas and doing Hollywood talk shows, so I thought I'd bring that Canadian talent here to celebrate them and show the world that our people went out and conquered the show business world but will always come back to this important place called the Imperial Room. I knew I had to bring top international acts in, too, and that was fine. And I knew audiences were expecting a bigger stage show for their buck in those days. Just an orchestra or a singer wasn't really enough. We needed to put on a show."

I asked Empry who the acts were that he thought were both Canadian and big enough to sustain a room with the reputation of the Imperial Room. "Well, Doug Henning was a guy who was wowing them from Las Vegas to London to Hollywood, a master magician and illusionist and a Canadian. The impressionist Rich Little was a regular in Hollywood on *The Tonight Show Starring Johnny Carson,* and, of course, Anne Murray, the wonderful Canadian songbird who had a couple of multi-gold records all over the world. They were the names I thought would be big enough to draw a Canadian crowd and who would be known by the people coming to the Imperial Room from the U.S. or Europe even."

But the razzle-dazzle of Vegas or the showbiz grandeur of Broadway didn't seem to fit at the Imperial Room despite the valiant efforts of Gino Empry. The Imperial Room wasn't designed for that kind of show, so audiences steadily declined until the place finally stopped being used as a nightclub.

It was during the Empry era that the Imperial Room saw Marlene Dietrich's swan song set of appearances to mark the end of her public performing career. A young bus boy at the Imperial Room, Bruce Bell (who is now recognized as an honorary historian for the hotel), remembers Dietrich from a personal encounter with the diva of all divas. "I found myself being summoned to clear some dishes away from her dressing room," says Bell. "I went in, and all of a sudden there she was! I mean, this was one of cinema's most legendary figures, and there I was in a smallish room with her. I started clearing the dishes into the bus pan when she asked me if I wanted a vodka tonic, so here I was, a star-struck bus boy in Toronto knocking back vodka tonics with Marlene Dietrich."

When pressed on the event, Bell recalls that Dietrich was very down-to-earth when hanging out one-on-one, but then she put on her costume, a skintight see-through dress and coat decorated with the breast feathers of 350 swans. "And then the myth was created," recounts Bell. "For an entire week I was allowed to follow the film goddess around like the excited little puppy I was."

The portrayal of Dietrich by Bell seems quite generous when measured alongside the descriptions of what needed to be done each and every time the singer/actress made her way to the Imperial Room dressing room before her shows. "She was escorted from her suite to a service elevator," Bell says, "then walked through the enormous kitchen to the backstage area of the Imperial Room. Staff had to line the walls of her walking route with posters and pictures of Dietrich posing from various films and performances when she was at her most glamorous." Bell says the reason for this was not just to show the staff and people in the hotel they were in the presence of one of the greatest stars, but also for the benefit of Dietrich herself, who was appearing onstage in a see-through outfit. Bell thinks that seeing herself so beautiful and glamorous before going on jacked her up and gave her a bit of added courage.

Jim Carrey, one of Canada's best-known comedians and actors, made his stage debut in the Imperial Room. He contorted himself, did wildly funny and deadly accurate impressions of everyone from Clint Eastwood to Jerry Lewis, and blew the assembled crowd away completely. A few years ago, in New York's Regency Hotel, I asked Carrey about his Imperial Room debut. By that time, Carrey was an A-list, $20-million-per-picture superstar.

"Do I remember it?" he asked me. "I'll never forget that night as long as I live! Everyone played that room, real big stars, and the place had a reputation not just for that but for the very discerning, sophisticated audiences it drew. And here I was bopping around the stage like a clown, hoping they wouldn't start throwing the silverware at me."

I asked Carrey if he remembered the reception he got. He became silent for a moment, then said, "It was fantastic. I felt like a real pro after that night. I felt like I could face any crowd, any audience, after that time at the Imperial Room. Maybe I wouldn't be sitting here today if I hadn't had that opportunity to impress and build my confidence as a performer."

The Imperial Room shifted gears and started playing host to a new collection of luminaries from a much different world. The

Empire Club used the room often for its meetings and speeches, many of which were televised. Since the Royal York first opened, the Empire Club had used the hotel as a meeting place, but not the Imperial Room specifically. The club is a Canadian speakers' forum that was started back in 1903 and is still going strong today. So instead of Jim Carrey and Tony Bennett drifting through the lobby to the Imperial Room, everyone from Indira Gandhi and the Dalai Lama to Bill Gates and Vladimir Putin sauntered through.

Many rooms in the Royal York have changed their purpose and function over the years, but as pomp and ceremony have always been part of the place, so, too, has a deep connection to culture. The C Floor Concert Hall is one of those rooms. It is as regal and grand as any room in any castle in Europe. This room was the location for the first ever performance of the Canadian Opera Company, and it also has a giant projection booth at one end that was used to show movies on a screen set up on the stage. The projection room and projector are no longer in use but are still in the enclosed area and are considered another couple of the truly historic artifacts that are quietly, almost secretly contained within the hotel's walls.

The Upper Canada Room on the 18th floor used to be the Tea Terrace. In fact, during the first decades of the Royal York's life, the 18th and 19th floors were really one big two-level tea room. Now the floors are separate and distinct again, and the Upper Canada Room is used for executive meetings.

As interesting as all the stories of dignitaries, royalty, sports heroes, and the odd scandal are, the things that make a great hotel truly great are the people who work the floors, tidy

The lobby of the Royal York, with its impressive clock and chandeliers, never ceases to awe first-time visitors.

the rooms, serve the meals, and answer questions. So when important dates in the life and times of the Royal York are being related, there are two dates and two names that need to be included, as well. One is March 6, 1986, the date when Bill Bilecki, a bellman, retired from the Royal York after more than 40 years of service. When Bilecki is asked what he considers the highlights of his time at the Royal York, he says, "It was the ordinary people I worked with every day. They made this job memorable."

The second important date is May 11, 1990, when Tony Hauth retired from his job as caterer at the Royal York after more than 50 years of service. While Hauth's father also worked at the Royal York, Tony started at the bottom. "I wasn't quite 16 years old when I started as a busboy," he says. "That was in 1940. And I was getting $35 a month plus what I could make in tips, and my meals were provided, so that was great also." It was Tony Hauth who cooked the meals for Queen Elizabeth II and Prince Philip during their 1973 visit to the Royal York, and for Hauth that occasion had an added bit of fun attached to it. "I'll never forget one day when Prince Philip caught four trout on a fishing trip. He popped down to the kitchen with them, gave them to me, and asked if they could be cooked for breakfast."

It is the Bill Bileckis and the Tony Hauths who make the Royal York the amazing place it is. Hauth describes the Royal York as the only place he has ever worked and the only place he ever wanted to work. That tells you something right there.

In 1997 *Wired* magazine featured a story about an urban mischief-maker who launched a 'zine and website called *Infiltration*. The whole point of this enterprise was to secretly invade a well-known building or place and report on the secrets that location holds. The technology magazine asked the shadowy urban infiltrator what the best place he ever infiltrated was and why. "The Royal York Hotel in Toronto, which was the focus of *Infiltration*'s first issue," he replied. "I honestly don't remember what first drew me to the Royal York, but something about it kept dragging me back week after week for about six months. It had free food and free drinks, free phone calls, comfy chairs, but even more tempting for me was the fact that beneath the incredibly polished, ritzy exterior hid a semi-secret world of narrow cement corridors, mysterious staircases, and unused attics. I started spending so much time at the Royal York that confused friends of mine kept asking me why the hell I kept going there, and when I told them why, I was amazed to find that they found it interesting, too. I found all this fascinating, of course, and was dying to write an article about all the neat things I uncovered. I couldn't think of any 'zine or magazine that would take such a submission, so I just decided to create one myself."

Upon further digging into "The Real Royal York," the title of the *Infiltration* piece, I discovered that the author, Ninjalicious (who passed away in 2005), was quite mistaken about a number of things. For instance, saying that a casual member of the public strolling into the hotel could have access to free food, drinks, and phone calls is more than a bit misleading. The free food and drinks are laid out for conventioneers or other officially accredited people attending events in the hotel. The average person isn't allowed to eat from those buffets unless his or her intention is to crash someone else's event. Free phone calls? Nowhere in the hotel can you make a free phone call unless you're using a house phone to call either one of the rooms or one of the services within the hotel.

Ninjalicious wrote that many security doors aren't alarmed despite notices that state they are, but he was wrong about that, too. There are certainly alarms on all the security doors, and such alarms go off in the security guards' headquarters in the hotel in what appears to be just another guest room.

Still Ninjalicious was right about one thing. The Royal York has fascinating secrets and boasts more than a few ghost stories. In fact, there are a number of lingering tales of mysterious phenomena that have persisted through the years. I made a conscious decision not to investigate those stories until I'd lived in the Royal York for at least a year or more. I wanted to see if I'd be visited by anything otherworldly or strange that I couldn't explain. That way, when I delved into the actual accounts of phantoms and bizarre occurrences, I could compare them to what I'd experienced myself.

As it turned out, two spine-chilling things happened to me in the Royal York that were reported by other people who had stayed in the hotel before me. Now to qualify my position on this whole thing up front, I don't refer to "ghosts" or "spirits" with any kind of fear or dread. I'm not entirely sure if such things are a part of our natural world, but if they are, I prefer to think of these transient spirits as guardian angels or lost souls rather than anything to be frightened of.

So here goes with my spectral encounters. Prior to a very cold Sunday evening in January 2010, I spent Saturday playing with Isabelle, my daughter. On Sunday, in the middle of the night, I woke up with something of a start. It was 3:36 a.m., and I could hear a little girl laughing and running up and down the hall. I assumed I'd been dreaming of Isabelle from the day before. As I lay there, I realized I was still hearing laughter and footfalls in the hall. It got louder and louder as if the little person were running deliriously up and down the hallway over and over again. Of course, I thought this was odd given the late hour, but "odd" can be commonplace in a busy hotel.

My first impression was that the child belonged to a family that had just flown in from Europe or some other far-off place and she was still operating on her body clock, not our time zone. When the laughter and running persisted, I got up to peer out the peephole in my door to see who the little girl was. As I squinted, I heard her laughing as she skipped toward my door. Her sounds drew nearer and nearer until she passed by my door, but there was no one in the hall! The noises then continued down the hall. I shook my head a bit and quietly opened the door. Glancing up and down the hallway, I saw there was no one in either direction. As for the sounds, they had abruptly ceased when I opened the door.

I pondered that night a couple of times but didn't feel I was actually touched by a paranormal phenomenon. Much later, however, when I was investigating mysterious happenings in the Royal York, I was told by an old doorman that, in fact, there had been complaints from guests dating back decades involving the laughter of children playing in the hallways during the late hours of the night. I was chilled to hear this particular story because it brought my own experience vividly to mind. Without a doubt I experienced a mixture of fear and excitement, but then I thought there was nothing to be afraid of. Instead, I reasoned, I should be grateful for having been touched by yet another unique aspect of the Royal York's astonishing history.

My second encounter with the unexplained occurred in July 2010. I had just finished my daily swim and was climbing into an elevator occupied by two old ladies. They were visiting from Kentucky (so said the name tags they were wearing for whatever event they were attending in the hotel). As we ascended, nothing was any different than countless other elevator rides

I'd taken in the Royal York. Then the elevator halted as if it had arrived at an appointed floor. But my floor was the first stop and we were still several floors away from that. Next, the lighted number indicating the floors went blank. It had been on seven, then ... nothing. Then an illuminated red sequence of three dashes appeared where the floor number should have been. One of the ladies commented, "Now this don't feel right a'tall."

I smiled and said it was a very old building, so the odd bit of idiosyncratic behaviour from the elevators was to be expected.

The other lady asked, "Well, what should we do? I'm claustrophobic."

I hit the open button, but nothing happened. A chilly gust of air blew into the elevator from the ornate wooden openings near the top of the car. I thought that was strange because it was like a blast furnace outside and even inside the air wasn't that cool. I wondered where the cold air had come from. I noticed that the claustrophobic lady from Kentucky had grasped the hand of the other woman. Then, as if nothing untoward had happened, the elevator started up again. This time it stopped at my floor. When the door opened, we all quickly exited and the Kentucky ladies headed over to call for another elevator. A few seconds later a member of the Royal York's security team came around the corner. I told him we had just been stuck in an elevator. The Kentucky women explained the incident. The security man asked which elevator, and we pointed at it. He said he would inform the maintenance people.

Later, when I was investigating the Royal York's spooky stories, I spoke to someone who had worked at the hotel since the 1970s but had retired in the late 1990s. He told me about little things like electrician's tools suddenly going dead even though there was nothing wrong with the circuits, or guests complaining to the front desk about being disturbed by lights in suites they could see from their windows going on and off, only to find out no guests were staying in those rooms.

The man then told me, "Elevators sometimes stop on a floor even though no one pushed the button for that floor. Then the doors open and there's this rush of cold air that comes in."

I shot the man a look. "Then what happens?"

He told me that nothing happened. A few seconds later the elevator would proceed as if nothing had occurred at all. While what was being related to me wasn't exactly the incident the Kentucky ladies and I had experienced, it was close enough to qualify as another bona fide inexplicable phenomenon.

Among the other legends of the Royal York's ghostly visitations are three that are very interesting indeed. Two even venture into Stephen King territory.

High in the upper reaches of the Royal York is the opulent Crystal Ballroom. It is another chandelier-adorned space that was for many years the very top of the town, a place where beautiful people came for spectacular parties. The Crystal Ballroom had to be closed because it failed to meet modern fire safety standards and because making alterations to comply with city codes was virtually impossible given the room's lofty position in the building. However, it seems that the thousands of revellers who enjoyed the Crystal Ballroom so thoroughly weren't prepared to let a few silly fire regulations spoil their fun. Long after the room was shuttered, the hotel's front desk got calls from guests staying on floors directly below. They complained about loud music and the sounds of large get-togethers going on above them well into the wee hours of the morning. On a number of occasions the guests, who weren't privy to the history of the place, got downright irate when they were informed there was no party taking place above them, since the ballroom wasn't being used anymore.

Then there is the elderly man in the burgundy smoking jacket and slippers who has been seen for decades strolling up and down the hallways of the eighth floor. Many people have reported spotting this man, and others have recounted the sighting to security or the front desk not out of fear or any kind of threat but because the man looks out of place and appears to be lost. Everyone who mentions this man describes him exactly the same way.

The rooms that house the Royal York's electrical equipment and elevator cables and engines, as well as the ancient stairways that lead to the roof, are generally off-limits. Of course, tours can be arranged in these areas of the hotel, and the roof has played host to a number of photo shoots involving rock stars or fashion models, but generally these parts of the Royal York are closed to the public and are covered by surveillance cameras for the sake of security and safety.

Many years ago a worker hanged himself in the stairwell leading to one of the highest points of the roof. This man was known to have emotional problems and then was accused of a rape and murder. Sadly, after he took his own life, the police arrested the person responsible for the crimes the worker had been accused of. Throughout the decades following the tragedy, electricians and other workers were frightened by loud cries and moans of agony issuing from the sealed-off sections and from the stairway leading to the roof. When the anxious complaints were made, a quick look at the tapes from the security cameras confirmed there was no one in the areas the workers claimed the unnerving noises were coming from. I've stood under the pipe where the worker hanged himself, and though I didn't hear or see anything out of the ordinary, I could see why the place might lend itself to people's imaginations.

One August afternoon in 2010 I finally decided it was time to crawl around in those dank, unused upper reaches of the

Royal York. The excursion was set up by Josh Stone, a Royal York health club attendant and my good friend, through Ryan, one of the engineers at the hotel. The Royal York's high attics sharply contrast with the opulence and beauty found in every public part of the hotel so much that you can't really believe the attics belong in the same building.

The high attic behind the neon Fairmont Royal York sign is a dark, cavernous space that would make a perfect setting for a horror movie even without the benefit of a set decorator. I noticed a rope hanging from the ceiling gently swaying back and forth as it had no doubt been doing for years undisturbed. We gained access to various levels of the roof through narrow, rusted staircases and tiny three-foot-by-three-foot doors that we had to crawl through, but it was worth it to be up there looking at the stone gargoyles and griffins watching over the hotel. It was an odd, somewhat serene sensation to stand on one of the uppermost roofs, knowing that beneath our feet the hotel operated at full tilt. And what was stranger still about crawling around in those unused nooks and crannies was that going through one door put you into the impressive Upper Canada Room and the palatial beauty of the 18th-floor rooms now used for meetings and official functions. The ghosts of the attics were only a few walls away.

The Royal York's upper off-limits floors and rooms are where one finds the muscles that have strained and tightened and flexed and kept the hotel strong and functioning all these years with very little in the way of upgrading or modernizing. When you stand beside the two giant rusted iron water tanks that supply fresh water to the entire hotel, you're gazing at the same tanks that workers saw eight decades ago. When you look at the huge elevator engines and cables, you marvel that they've been in almost constant motion for more than 80 years.

When you walk around the empty rooms that once functioned as workshops for silversmiths, you wonder what those rooms must have been like decades ago when they were plying their trade daily in the upper reaches of the hotel. The history you don't feel and absorb throughout the hotel is stored here where it is quiet and where time seems to have stood still for decades.

Often throughout this book I have and will refer to the effect of the collective energies that have been expended within the Royal York's walls by so many varied characters and how the wonderful atmosphere of the hotel is partly due to those energies swirling unseen in its interior. So if you come to the Royal York to stay and are assigned a suite on the eighth floor, keep an eye out for an older guy in a burgundy smoking jacket and slippers pacing your hall, but don't fear him. After all, he is probably just a guy like me, someone who checked into the Royal York one day and never left.

Speaking of swirling energies, a couple of the longer-serving maids at the Royal York told me about a ghostly spectre in a white translucent gown who appears in only two suites — the high corner 15-150 and 16-150. Some of the maids and room attendants are said to be too nervous to go into these suites alone because of the stories. I asked the maids if either of them had seen this apparition. Neither had, but they had heard tales from other maids who had.

I had one other very eerie thing happen to me, a sort of *Twilight Zone* incident that conjured up Rod Serling's voice saying something like: "On this morning Mr. Christopher Heard stepped out of his suite in the Fairmont Royal York Hotel and into the Twilight Zone …" I was finished my daily swim, had showered off the chlorine, and was getting dressed to head out for a coffee before my writing day began. The phone rang. It was the front desk. An urgent young female voice asked, "Mr. Heard, are you all right?" Not having a clue what she meant, I told her I was fine. She persisted. "Are you sure you're all right? We can send someone up right away if you need help."

I chuckled and told her she had made a mistake or gotten her lines crossed somehow. I was fine and didn't need help. She then told me that the front desk had received a call from my suite and that someone with a voice like mine had urgently requested medical assistance. While finding all this quite odd, I assured her I had never felt better and had made no such plea. She hung up, but I had the impression she still wasn't convinced.

When I finished dressing, I headed for the door, only to hear someone knock on it. I opened the door and discovered a Fairmont security man there. "Mr. Heard, just checking to see that you're okay." I told him I was fine, as he could plainly see. He then told me that a second distress call had been made from my suite by someone with a voice similar to mine. I assured him I had made no such call either time and that I was perfectly fine. Then I swung the door open and asked him to have a look. "That won't be necessary, sir. I just needed to see if you're okay."

"No, no," I said. "I want you to come in and look around so you can report there's nothing out of the ordinary or untoward going on here should another such call be made."

He entered, glanced around, and nodded. "Thanks. I'm glad you're all right."

"Me, too," I said.

For the rest of that day I thought about those weird phone calls. Every time I pondered them the theme from *The Twilight Zone* played in my head: *"Do,do,do,do ... do, do, do, do ..."*

We live in a time when environmental awareness is not only admirable but downright essential. Generally speaking, corporate civic and environmental responsibility is usually done for the sole reason of achieving favourable public relations, but the Royal York has always been a place of energy conservation and environmental awareness because it chooses to and because it makes good sense. Recycling and being "green" enhances and improves the operation of a hotel the size of a small town in all sorts of ways. The Royal York's rooftop herb and vegetable garden not only supplies fresh ingredients for the kitchen but is also used as a draw for guests. A stay-package at the hotel provides guests with visits to the herb garden and also allows them to accompany one of the chefs to nearby St. Lawrence Market to select locally grown produce for the kitchen.

With an enterprise the size of the Royal York there is always the problem of potentially wasting a mountain of food every day. It is estimated that the hotel produces about 2,200 pounds of food waste per day, all of which is picked up daily by Turtle Island Recycling for composting. Food that isn't consumed at banquets and events is given to Second Harvest, which distributes it to more than 27 agencies that feed the needy. Every year the Royal York also donates more than 20,000 pounds of soap and 4,000 pounds of shampoo to various missions and social agencies. The hotel also donates a considerable number of bedsheets and pillowcases. Other aspects of conservation and environmental protection include the cutting of gas consumption by almost 50 percent over the past 20 years, something that was simply done by eliminating a waste incinerator and turning off all kitchen equipment and apparatus when not in use; the reprocessing of 300,000 pounds of cardboard and paper each year, the equivalent of 4,000 trees still standing that would have otherwise been cut down; and the recycling of 400,000 glass bottles annually.

Living in a hotel as a permanent resident was always a carefully held and nurtured dream of mine. When the time, circumstances, and elements aligned, I knew the Royal York was the only place where I could realize my dream. Since I was literally conceived in the Royal York, my connection to it borders on the cosmic. And strangely, because I was only told of this fact later in life, the knowledge of my conception brought everything in my life into sharper focus. All of a sudden I understood why I seemed drawn to the Royal York, why I often sat in a mezzanine lounge chair to read or write when I had a few spare minutes in Toronto, why I immediately thought of the hotel when I was searching for a location to do interviews, even though there were other, more convenient hotels offering their spaces to me for that purpose. When my father confirmed for me that my history and the saga of the Royal York were inextricably linked, the future course of my life became crystal clear.

BOOK THREE

SUITE DREAMS

T HREE PEOPLE WERE KEY FIGURES IN my becoming writer-in-residence at The Fairmont Royal York Hotel: Mike Taylor, Fairmont public relations director and my long-time friend; Melanie Coates, Fairmont's regional marketing manager; and Heather McCrory, Fairmont's regional vice-president and the Royal York's general manager. In early June 2009, I moved into a suite in the Royal York that was just perfect — not overly huge, not too small. It has a bedroom area that's roomy and comfortable and a living room section with a sofa, a chair, and a coffee table. The room also contains a desk in front of one of the two windows, and the ceiling is high, giving the space an airy, open feeling.

The first morning I woke up in my room I spied a stoic stone griffin outside. The morning sunshine washed over the griffin, and the sand-coloured stone of the hotel dramatically contrasted with the TD Waterhouse tower's black glass and steel just beyond. I lay there gazing at that griffin and had an epiphany: the griffin guarding the Royal York from just outside my window strangely would symbolize my entire hotel-living experience. The new life I was embarking on would be as real as the stone the griffin was carved from, but at the same time otherworldly. A book on hotel living and culture was always something I felt I was working toward. On that first morning, regarding my new guardian jutting from a corner of the hotel, I knew I had begun the book you are now reading. I didn't have a title and didn't know what adventures and stories were to come, but I knew the image of the griffin was special. Since then a day hasn't passed that I haven't looked out at that griffin at least once.

During those early days as a hotel resident, I quickly realized that when you live in a hotel you have to make certain adjustments. It is impossible to be a pack rat in a hotel. Previously, as a confirmed magazine junkie, I let periodicals pile up everywhere. When you live in a hotel, though, you don't have space for that sort of thing. So now, when a new copy of a favourite magazine comes out, I recycle the previous one. The same is true with clothes. These days I don't buy clothing simply because I think it might look good, since I know I don't have the space for such indulgences. As for books, I still have them heaped on end tables and on my desk, but not to the degree I did before moving into the Royal York. On the walls in a couple of areas I openly display my daughter Isabelle's latest works of art, but beyond that life as a hotel resident forces me to practise a wonderful sort of minimalism that strips away a lot of clutter. And that lack of litter and disorder allows me more time to do other things.

Let's face it. I don't spend a lot of energy searching for things since everything is pretty well ready to hand. I also don't do a lot of tidying up because everything is usually in its place by natural arrangement. As an additional benefit, because maids and other hotel people, say, those who wash the windows or change air filters or the batteries in the smoke alarms, are free to enter my suite whenever they need to, I know that if I don't keep the place neat the people I share this building with will think I'm a slob.

I had arranged, through my editor/webmaster friend, Andrew Powell, to do a ten-part serial on the early days of my new life as a hotel resident for TheGate.ca, the entertainment/lifestyle website he runs. I was asked to deliver a thousand words or so every ten days chronicling that period. As a further plus, this arrangement would be a good way to try out material that would ultimately find its way into this book only in a more expanded form. I decided I would first examine all the aspects that fascinated me about hotel living and culture and see if other people shared the same or similar views of them. Pretty quickly, as it turned out, I learned that romance and sex were uppermost in the minds of most of my fellow hotel residents.

There is something deeply romantic and sensual about hotels, especially old ones with the lingering energy of decades of adventure contained within their walls. One of the things you notice when you live in a hotel is that people coming and going for conventions, meetings, or events of one kind or another act differently than when they are at home. They are noticeably less inhibited and give off an aura that broadcasts that to the world. Generally speaking, they are more talkative and adventurous because they are away from their routine and are in a place of comfort and luxury.

Aside from my direct personal experience, and yes, I can confirm that sex in the Royal York is as fantastic as it gets, I discovered that many people I casually asked about romance and sex opened up about them without much hesitation, especially while sipping cognac or other spirits in either the Library Bar or EPIC. Romantic sex, quickie sex, unexpected, spontaneous sex, first-time sex, reconnecting sex all happen on a nightly (and daily) basis at the Royal York and every other luxury hotel of note.

Once I realized people would openly talk about sex and romance within the Royal York's walls, I decided to interview individuals, with great delicacy, on those very topics. I always identified myself as an author and made sure that sex and romance in the Royal York weren't the first things I brought up in conversation. Amazingly, not a single person refused to discuss the subjects. Many people even recounted in great detail and with giddy enthusiasm romantic adventures they'd had in the Royal York.

One such chat began on a bone-chillingly cold evening in February in the Library Bar. I was sitting alone sipping Hennessey, something I did often during the writing of this book. On this particular evening I was seated next to a gentleman who was one couch over. He was alone but clearly waiting for someone. As I enjoyed the Library Bar's atmosphere, a lovely young woman approached me. The lady was a flight attendant with a large British carrier. She mentioned that she recognized me from the last time she was in town a month or so earlier. I told her it wasn't the coincidence she assumed, since I lived in the Royal York. A brief, awkward exchange followed; she was clearly at least two glasses of wine over the tipping point. Finally, she said it was time to go up and get into her "jammies." Casually, she reached for my notebook, wrote her room number on a blank page, and said she would be awake for another couple of hours if I wanted to "drop up" to continue the conversation.

When she left, the gentleman to my right slid a bit closer with a smile and made a remark having to do with what I had just passed up. I told him she'd had a bit too much to drink and I would hate myself in the morning if I took advantage of that for a number of reasons, not the least of which was I already had a lovely woman to share that kind of fun with. Then he said, "Funny how you just naturally feel sexier in this place." That interested me. I introduced myself to him and explained that I resided in the Royal York and was working on a book about hotel living. I inquired if I could ask him about what he'd meant by his remark — on the record. He said sure, but he asked that his full name not be used. So I'll call him Al.

Al went on to explain that he was an executive with a southwestern Ontario whiskey company. He had been working nonstop for a couple of years, and his wife, let's call her Kathy, had been doing the same. They decided to book time off to come to the Royal York for a Friday-through-Sunday getaway weekend. They would have a nice dinner at Benihana's, see a show, and make love the way they had twenty years earlier.

The days leading up to the trip to Toronto had them exchanging playfully suggestive emails and leaving naughty notes in each other's pockets, so when they checked into the hotel, they had already built up tangible excitement for the experience at hand. "We got inside the suite, put our bags down, and stretched out on the huge bed and relaxed," Al told me. "Then you know what? We just started making out like we were a couple of teenagers. It was great! Then we decided to really go for it, right then and there in the afternoon. I put the PRIVACY PLEASE sign on the door and we did it. The last time we did it in the afternoon was ... never."

I had to remind Al a couple of times that I was, in fact, writing notes on his experience. I asked Al what he attributed the sudden excitement to. "Well, we're both in good shape, we both work out and eat well, we both have lots of energy, so our lack of contact in that department was simply because we allowed ourselves to get way too busy, so there was no time. We both started to worry that we'd actually grown apart and lost interest in each other, so we decided to come here, forget everything else, and enjoy each other for a few days."

I asked him if he picked the Royal York for any specific reason. "We've both stayed here before on business, but never together, so we thought it would be perfect because we were both familiar with the place but not familiar with each other being here."

I agreed with Al that the class and charm that are part of every inch of the Royal York is really lost on most newer hotels, which are half hotel, half condo, with the condo part taking priority. The Royal York, on the other hand, is the way great hotels used to be, should still be.

Al continued his recollection of the past 36 hours or so by saying, "Once we started we didn't want to stop. We did it in the bed, we did it in the shower, we even did it spontaneously against the door as soon as it closed behind us last night after we got back from dinner!"

I asked him what he thought the larger meaning of all this was, and he sat back and thought for a moment. "I'll tell you, this place just makes you feel ... good, about everything, about simple things. This is a place where you're allowed to relax and slow down if you choose. I don't love Kathy any more than I did, but coming to this place just allowed us to leave everything else behind and focus on that."

Just then his wife, Kathy, stepped into the Library Bar. She was a tall, slim, very attractive woman in her late fifties with a shimmering mane of silver hair. As she walked over to join her husband, I looked at her in a much different way than I would have had I not just chatted with her husband. She was a vibrant, beautiful, sexy woman. Al introduced me to his wife, and we exchanged a few pleasantries. Then I excused myself because I didn't want to take even a moment away from them.

A similar, wonderfully inspiring story that was related to me also happened in the Library Bar. Strangely, I wasn't the one who initiated the discussion. While I sipped my drink and made notes, a couple sitting next to me were enjoying their Bloody Caesars. They were about to head over to EPIC for dinner and were checking out the Library Bar they'd heard so much about. The woman, in her early fifties, kept glancing at me. Then she smiled and asked if I was the fellow who appeared on Michael Coren's television show regularly to talk about pop culture events of the week. I said I was, and they both mentioned that they had heard Coren talking to me about living in the Royal York. I told them what I was doing and asked them what had brought them to the hotel. The woman said, "This is our 25th anniversary, and we had to spend it here because we were married in the Royal York and spent our wedding night here."

I told her that their story was repeated many times each year at the Royal York. The man said, "Our story is a bit different because we always felt cheated out of the fun of a wild and sexy wedding night. We promised each other we would one day come back here and live the passionate, unbridled wedding night we were denied the first time around."

I didn't know if I should inquire further about what had happened that first night a quarter-century ago, but the woman filled in the story for me without my having to ask. "The wedding was done, the reception was all but over, then two of our friends from out in the country, who had never been to Toronto before, wanted to do something they always wanted to do — get a hot dog from the wagon in front of Union Station. Because they were leaving, we said we would join them, so we excused ourselves and ran across the street for hot dogs. They were delicious, but they also poisoned us!"

The man added, "So because we had never actually, you know, done it, we had been really looking forward to that night, as you can well imagine. But we didn't even get into our suite before we both began having severe cramps and ended up violently ill."

The woman laughed and shook her head at the memory. "We spent the night running back and forth to the bathroom, cold sweats, looking and feeling like the wrath of God, not exactly conducive to you know what."

I expressed my condolences, then the man explained they had promised each other that one weekend they would come back here to the Royal York and enjoy that night as if it were the first.

I asked if tonight was the night, and the woman chuckled. "Oh, no, we took care of that last night!"

"And this morning," the man added.

I asked if it was everything they'd hoped and imagined. "It was better, much better," the woman said. "We had 25 years of experience, so this time we really knew what we were doing, something neither of us could have said that first night."

"So, you know, we couldn't say it was our first time, but we can sure say it was our best time!" the man said. He took his wife's hand and squeezed it. They shared a smile that told me that even though the bar was packed and it was quite noisy, they were alone and back in their suite enjoying each other, not caring a lick who was watching. That's the kind of magic the Royal York can produce in even those who least expect it.

The other end of the scale was represented one morning by a young couple who appeared to be in their late twenties. It was Sunday morning, and I was in York's Kitchen enjoying another of their fabulous made-to-order omelettes before heading out to do my weekly radio spot. The young couple seated beside me along the back wall just east of the buffet area was clearly on a honeymoon. They were both eating large plates of eggs, potatoes, and bacon from the buffet, while I was having my usual Swiss cheese, asparagus, and tomato omelette. I had to contain my laughter as the attractive, talkative young woman said things between bites like: "I can barely walk this morning, and the muscles on the insides of my thighs are so stiff it hurts to walk." A few mouthfuls later she added: "The bed in our suite is big enough and wide enough that we can try that position I was telling you about, the one I read about in *Cosmopolitan*."

This was one of the few times I actively tried not to listen to a story. Then the woman shovelled half a slice of toast into her mouth, mock-shivered, and said, "Ooooh, I just want to stay naked with you all day long! Let's go back up to ten [their floor] before heading out this morning. I haven't had enough of you yet!"

By this time I was shielding the side of my face with my fingers as I snickered at each word she uttered. Then it dawned on me that while the woman was unable to contain her comments, the man hadn't said a single word in reply. Instead he smiled and winked at her, eating wordlessly. It was another confirmation of my theory that people become who they imagine themselves to be in big hotels like the Royal York. This woman was saying what she was thinking because she felt like it and there was no one there to judge her because no one knew her there. She was completely anonymous, a stranger to everyone except her husband. This time in this place existed outside their normal lives. They finished breakfast and quickly signed the bill before leaving. I noticed she was limping noticeably and snickered again. She was so sexed up she was having trouble walking! The uncensored, uninhibited display was both funny and wonderful to see.

That lowering of inhibitions sometimes shows up in the strangest places and at the most unexpected times. My daily routine includes a one-hour swim in the health club pool each morning. It is a ritual that is as much a part of my day as eating. If I slip into the pool at 6:30 a.m., I get out at 7:30, one hour later, no exceptions. Depending on my timing and the occupancy rate of the hotel, I either swim my hour completely alone or I have to swim an obstacle course around other people doing morning laps.

In early February 2010 a collection of teachers was in the hotel for a union meeting/convention. Hundreds of teachers

The Royal York's swimming pool in the hotel's health club is where I do my laps every morning.

(Courtesy Fairmont Hotels & Resorts)

from all over Ontario descended on the hotel, most of them women. So for that four-day stretch the pool was filled with young women, older women, all shapes and sizes of women from the time the pool opened at 6:00 a.m. until it came time for the breakfast meetings and seminars to begin. Every morning I found myself swimming laps beside and between women who were away from home and enjoying the freedom and comfort of the Royal York.

One morning I timed it out so that when I was getting into the pool most of the teachers were on their way out. After a few minutes of swimming, it was just one teacher and me swimming laps. She was in her thirties and wore a relaxed smile as she swam. We shared a couple of smiles as we passed each other on laps but didn't actually exchange a word. She climbed out of the water and walked over to where her towel and robe were on a lounge chair next to the hot tub beside the pool. Drying herself off, she casually removed her one-piece bathing suit, stepped out of it, and stood naked for a few moments in full view. Then she bent for her robe, slipped it on, and tied the belt around her waist. Picking up her bathing suit and towel, she strolled out of the health club.

Instantly, I thought, *Would she have done that anywhere else but here?* My question was sort of answered a few hours later. I was going out for something to eat when I passed my bathing-beauty friend. Amazingly, she was dressed as conservatively as can be imagined in a dark brown pinstriped pantsuit with her hair tightly done up in a bun. She looked like the stereotypical New England schoolmarm of song and story. I smiled all the way to the deli at how this buttoned-down woman, a teacher, felt the sensual pull of the Royal York and went with it to the point of stripping off her swimsuit and allowing me to gaze at her naked body in a semi-public setting.

Then I wondered to myself: *Was that woman in the lobby the real her, or was the woman in the pool who felt sexy and sensual enough to be naked before a man, a stranger, the real her?* I regret not going up to her to suggest we discuss the question philosophically over coffee, but doing that would have torn the thin gauze of mystique that she had wrapped herself in.

Whenever I reveal that I live in the Royal York, the bandwidth of reactions I get ranges from expressions of interest and curious speculation to a wide variety of comments about movies or books famous for featuring hotels. On a number of occasions I've been referred to as Norman Bates. However, that allusion isn't entirely accurate. In Alfred Hitchcock's *Psycho*, Bates owns a motel not a hotel, and he doesn't live in it; he resides in a house on the hill behind the motel with his dead mother. Another popular comparison is, of course, Eloise, a suggestion nearer to the mark. As I mentioned earlier in this book, Eloise is the child who lives in the Plaza Hotel in New York City. The obvious main difference there is that Eloise is a little girl and I'm a semi-grown-up man.

Then there's Jack Torrance, the closest analogy of all. Torrance is the protagonist in Stephen King's novel *The Shining* (as well as in the Stanley Kubrick movie and the TV miniseries) as I detailed in Book One. In King's novel Torrance is a writer living in the Overlook Hotel in Colorado's Rocky Mountains. The hotel is closed during the winter months, and Torrance has been hired as the caretaker. Slowly, he descends into madness inspired by the evil that lives in the old hotel, which we learn has pulled him psychically to the place.

Of course, my experience is the complete opposite to Torrance's. Jack's writing output during his time in the Overlook consists of a few thousand pages of writing "All work and no play makes Jack a dull boy," while I've written three books back to back with a fourth underway during my time at the Royal York. But in December 2009 something happened that actually made me feel as if I were Jack Torrance and that I'd been surreally transported into the pages of *The Shining*.

The morning began as it always did. I woke up ridiculously early, did some stretching, took a mitt full of vitamins, then padded off to the pool to talk to Josh Stone and swim my usual laps. Only this particular morning something wasn't right, something seemed odd. Not bad, just not as I'd come to feel things commonly. As I walked down the hallway to the elevator bank, the sensation grew, but as soon as I hit the pool, I forgot all about it. Heading back to my suite after being invigorated by the swim, I was hit with the mood again. Something was amiss, but once more I couldn't identify what was bothering me. So I did my day's worth of writing on the book I was working on at the time and didn't think too much more about it.

In the early evening I answered a knock. A Fairmont executive was there when I opened the door. She told me I didn't have to worry. If I needed anything at all, I was only a call downstairs away. I was completely puzzled by her assurance. I'd been living in the Royal York for several months, and while I rarely called downstairs for anything, I knew that was always an option. I think the executive could see the slight confusion on my face because she then said, "You're all alone."

This statement merely added another layer of befuddlement. Thinking she might be speaking existentially, I replied, "Well, aren't we all."

She laughed, then explained that due to seasonally low occupancy rates the hotel closed a few floors so the maids didn't have to hustle their big rigs more than they needed to. So, I was told, I would be alone on my floor throughout December.

I told the executive that the maids could come up once every four or five days and that I would take care of everything else myself. The Fairmont woman then said I should enjoy the solitude and get lots of writing done. Soon after I did start feeling very alone.

The next morning, when I stepped out to go for my swim, the quiet, the lack of newspapers waiting outside doors, the absence of sounds as I padded down the hallway (women drying their hair, CNN blaring from televisions) was eerie and exactly why I'd experienced the odd sensation the day before. After a week or so of this isolation, I began to get antsy, the already long hallways seemed even longer, and the silence was deafening. I even had a dream one night that I went down to the lobby and it was deserted, too. I was truly isolated in the giant hotel. After that I found myself drifting down to the lobby to make sure there was still activity going on. When the regular team of maids returned to my floor in January, I told them how much I'd missed them, and it was their turn to look bewildered.

Something that obviously sets hotel living apart from residing in a condo or a house in a regular tree-lined neighbourhood is the fact that, first, your neighbours change a couple of times per week, and second, you never know who you're going to have in your midst. Sometimes the people whose paths you cross inspire magical moments. One Sunday morning I was getting ready to leave and do my weekly radio show when the maid stopped by to do her thing. Departing early to let her finish, I went down to the lobby and spotted someone I recognized instantly. I hadn't met him before, so I wasn't sure how to approach him. Taking a deep breath, I stepped over to him and said, "Excuse me, Mr. Islam?"

In a resonant, British-accented voice he replied, "Yes, indeed."

I extended a hand and told him I was an enormous fan of his music and that from the time I was a teenager his music had been a source of inspiration to me. He took my hand with both of his, smiled, and thanked me for being so gracious, then said he was meeting friends for breakfast at EPIC and could I walk with him as he went. This man was once known as Cat Stevens, a legendary pop/rock balladeer who scored one major hit after another in the early 1970s, from "Peace Train" and the haunting "King of Trees" to the inspirational "If You Want to Sing Out, Sing Out" (which Apple commandeered for its iPhone commercials). The life of a rock star lost its meaning for him, and he converted to Islam, changed his name to Yusuf Islam, and gave away much of his wealth to charity. Yusuf was in town to play at a festival celebrating the positive aspects of Islam. We chatted amiably as we strolled through the lobby to the entrance of EPIC where he met a group of friends. As I was leaving him, I said, "I think you're one of the greatest singer/songwriters ever."

He smiled, waved, and said, "There you go being gracious again. Thank you."

As I continued to the exit I kept thinking, *I was just chatting with Cat Stevens.* The truly interesting thing, however, is that it could only have happened at the Royal York, and if the maid hadn't come by exactly when she did, I wouldn't have been in the lobby as Stevens walked to breakfast. That kind of happenstance meeting with interesting characters is almost as commonplace as the organized interviews with fascinating people I've had the good fortune to conduct within the walls of the Royal York.

During the 2009 edition of the Toronto International Film Festival, which the Royal York is an active participant in through the tireless work of film and television liaison Kolene Elliott, living in the Royal York meant running into actors and directors constantly during the ten-day event. Some I was acquainted with from previous encounters or interviews, while others were new to me. For example, I ran into Irish actor Brendan Gleeson in the lobby. We had met before, and I congratulated him on his Emmy nomination for playing Winston Churchill and asked if he thought he would win. "Are you fooking kidding?" Gleeson said. "I'm up against fooking Jack Bauer, aren't I?" A week later Gleeson won the Emmy, and Jack Bauer (Kiefer Sutherland's role in 24) didn't.

One of the funniest encounters I've had with a film festival visitor was with British funnyman Ricky Gervais. He was in the Royal York promoting his festival film *The Invention of Lying,* and we shared an elevator together one morning. We talked about the Old World elegance of the hotel, and I told him I lived in the Royal York. Moreover I was actually conceived in the hotel. He smiled and asked, "Wot, and you just never left?"

"Yes, something like that," I replied.

Just after the film festival finished for another year, I was strolling through the lobby after dinner and was about to take a stroll down to Harbourfront. It was an extraordinarily warm September evening. As I headed out the front door, a young couple stopped me. One of them had a tourist map in his hands. "Excuse me," the man, Cody, asked me. "I've seen you around the hotel. Do you know your way around this town?" I told him I lived in the hotel and asked how I might help them. "We're trying to figure out if Harbourfront is walking distance from here or if we should hop in a cab," he said. I told them not only was it walking distance but I was on my way there myself and could accompany them.

As we sauntered south on York Street, I gave the couple a thumbnail history of the Royal York. In a stroke of sheer coincidence the woman, Sharon, asked if I'd written anything online about how magical the Royal York was. She was describing one of the articles I'd done for TheGate.ca, a piece that had been picked up by Google News. I told her I'd written a series of online articles as part of a larger book-length project. They then complimented me by telling me it was that piece that convinced them the Royal York was the kind of place they not only wanted to go to but needed to go to.

At first I found that an odd way of putting it, but I eventually learned why it wasn't strange at all. As we walked, they told me they were from Ohio and had been married for three years, but unfortunately they had hardly seen each other for the past two and were using this long weekend to reconnect. I asked if work had separated them all that time.

"Something like that, yeah," Cody said. "We've both just been rotated home. We've been deployed for the past two years."

It turned out they were U.S. soldiers. Sharon was connected to a unit in Kirkuk, and Cody was an infantryman who had spent two years patrolling in Tikrit. I noticed the insignia tattooed inside Cody's right forearm and assumed it was his unit's symbol.

Brimming with questions, I marvelled at how these two young married people had had to put their lives together as a couple aside for years so they could go off to an ancient foreign land to fight a war no one really understood, a violent, bloody, at times savage conflict that both were lucky to survive. However, I kept my questions to myself, remembering what Cody had told me about the Royal York being a place they "needed" to come to. They were here not to tell me war stories, not to relive things better left to drift; they were here for the quiet, the calm, the freedom, and to forget the recent past and focus on what was to come.

All I could say was: "Wow, every day will be sweet from here on in for you guys. You made it!" Instantly, I knew I'd said the wrong thing. They both looked at me awkwardly. They were carrying a lot of bad stuff deep inside, things they'd seen, perhaps things they'd had to do, so achieving "sweet" would take a while. More time would have to pass for them to reach that state.

When we arrived at Harbourfront, I gave them a quick description of where the attractions were, then told them to enjoy their evening together. They both shook hands with me and thanked me. I said it was my pleasure and that they might even turn up in the next essay I wrote about life in the Royal York.

As we parted, I thought about Sharon's handshake. Her hands were rough and her handshake was firm, almost as much as Cody's. These people, who looked to be on the sunny side of 25, were in need of some magic, so I reminded them that they had picked the right place to hang out for it.

My familiarity with the Royal York is long and personal, but it is also born of a professional relationship I have with the place. Throughout my years as an interviewer, both on TV and in print, whenever I was offered an author, movie star, or director for an interview, I always suggested, if it weren't in a set, established location, that the chat be conducted at the Royal York. Whether it be one of my favourite Canadian actors Don McKellar or a veteran maverick filmmaker such as Arthur Penn (*Bonnie and Clyde*), whenever I confirmed an interview I got in touch with either Fairmont's Mike Taylor or Melanie Coates to set up the location in the hotel. This must have occurred a hundred times or more over the years.

Of the organized interviews I've done in the Royal York there are two that stand out above the rest. One was with Karl Malden. The interview with Malden was arranged because the actor was in town to plug his then recently published memoir *When Do I Start?* The publisher's public relations person was having trouble drumming up interest for some reason, but being a film historian I was completely and utterly intrigued with the prospect of talking to such a distinguished thespian.

The plan was to shoot the interview in a park, but I was to meet Malden first in the mezzanine lounge of the Royal York. After I greeted the actor, we talked about his experiences onstage with a very young, inexperienced Marlon Brando during the first Broadway run of *A Streetcar Named Desire*, then moved on to all the film work he'd done with Brando and all the movies he'd acted in with virtually every other big-name actor and director of his era.

Malden told me about sitting on a movie set in a desert area of Spain doubling for Second World War North Africa. The film was *Patton*, and Malden recalled a blazing hot day under a makeshift tent with George C. Scott, who wore his full Patton uniform (Malden was General Omar Bradley). Malden got up and went out to survey the set, gazing at the tanks and the extras dressed as soldiers in that bleak, sun-blasted setting. He tried to imagine what it must have been like for those soldiers in that alien landscape during the Second World War, knowing they were about to face Erwin Rommel and his tanks coming at them from somewhere in the shimmering distance. Then Malden told me the mood was shattered when he heard Scott bellow, "Karl, you goddamn son of a bitch, are we going to play chess or not?"

While Malden and I sat in the mezzanine lounge, a number of passersby recognized the actor, but no one bothered us. The attention prompted me to ask Malden what his most awkward encounter with a fan was. He chuckled because he had a very specific story. Malden was of Serbian descent. His name was actually Mladen George Sekulovich. He had changed it when he became an actor. During a visit to the former Yugoslavia after becoming a well-known movie star and winning an Oscar for best supporting actor in *A Streetcar Named Desire*, Malden spent some time at a nude beach on the resort island of Hvar off the coast of Croatia.

"There I was on this beautiful beach as naked as the day I was born," Malden said, "when up walks a German woman who was quite obviously as naked as the day she was born. She asked me for my autograph. I was a bit taken aback and wondered why I had to explain what couldn't have been more obvious. She didn't have anything for me to sign, and I didn't have anything to sign it with!"

Karl Malden (1912–2009) won a best supporting actor Oscar in 1951 for his portrayal of Mitch in A Streetcar Named Desire.

The second truly memorable Royal York interview was with Hong Kong action star Jackie Chan. I had interviewed Jackie a few times over the years and had always found him generous and gracious. Jackie was even kind enough to read my book on Hong Kong film director John Woo (it was Woo who first gave Chan a starring role) and write a nice endorsement for the back cover. In the fall of 2001, Jackie was in Toronto to shoot his newest film, *The Tuxedo*, at the Royal York (and in my hometown of Oshawa). So I joined him in a hotel suite for what turned out to be a wild interview.

Jackie Chan is a wonderful guy to spend time with. He is friendly and infuses every moment with an infectious, positive energy. After we spoke enthusiastically about our mutual love of old Hollywood musicals (one of his favourites, *Singin' in the Rain*; one of mine, *Guys and Dolls*), we turned our chat to the topic of choreographing action and fight scenes and explored the idea that dance and fight scenes follow similar principles. I asked Jackie if he could demonstrate how a fight scene evolved. Did he have a finale in mind that he worked backward from, or did physics dictate what was required to choreograph a fight scene from start to finish?

From our previous conversations Jackie knew I had some martial arts experience of my own, so he knew I could throw a punch, kick, and block.

"Give me one punch, then another fast right after," he said.

I did as instructed and was astonished at his reaction. Jackie blocked one punch, then threw himself backward to dodge the second, landing in a chair behind him, which fell over. Then he rolled out of the toppled chair and into a standing position.

We did this a few more times, then he said again, "Give me one punch."

I threw a punch but varied it without thinking. Jackie blocked my blow and threw a lightning-fast counterpunch, but because I'd stepped toward him I'd thrown his timing and judgment of the distance off. The back of his fist cracked hard against my forehead above my right eye. Because of the angle of the punch (and the fact that I'm six foot four), my head snapped downward and my chin hit my chest. As I raised my head, I felt a throbbing pain in my forehead and saw a galaxy of swirling pinpricks of light.

Before I could fall like a chain-sawed tree, Jackie grabbed my sweater and lowered me to the sofa, apologizing profusely. He said something rapidly but calmly in Cantonese to one of his assistants, who quickly stepped out of the room. The movie production company's public relations person, a lovely young girl, looked on in horror. I figured that meant Jackie had rearranged my features substantially. Jackie's assistant returned with ice in a hand towel, which Jackie pressed to my eye and forehead. He said sorry repeatedly while I told him everything was my fault, all the while thinking, *I was just slugged by Jackie Chan! How many other writers can lay claim to that distinction?*

With each moment that the ice was pressed to my face, I got more coherent. By the time I left the suite, I could walk more or less. The blow to my forehead hadn't broken the skin, but for the next 24 hours or so I looked more like a unicorn than a homo sapien.

Not all of my Royal York encounters with film people are as life-threatening as the one with Jackie Chan. Over the years I've had many less strenuous movie conversations in the hotel. One evening in late July 2009 my friend Peter Miskimmin, producer and director of development with actor/director Paul Gross's Whizbang Films, stopped by for a drink and conversation at EPIC. Sitting at the outer railing so we could watch the comings and goings in the lobby, we talked for hours about one of our favourite subjects — the movies of the 1970s, the last great epoch of American cinema. Under producer Philip D'Antoni (who also produced *Bullitt* starring Steve McQueen), Pete worked in New York on *The French Connection*. While we were waiting for round two of our drinks to arrive, Pete looked around the lobby. "Being in this place always reminds me of Christmas," he said. I asked him why. "I would come here a lot over the years at Christmastime when it was all decorated up, so now whenever I see a picture of this place or find myself here it feels like Christmas to me."

I found that comment interesting because I realized that sense memory is common where hotels are concerned. Whenever a great hotel I've been in is mentioned to me, I immediately associate it with what I was doing when I stayed there, as if the hotel were a person I had some great adventure with. When round two arrived, Pete sipped his beer, I sipped my cognac, and we went back to talking about *Badlands*, *Dog Day Afternoon*, *The Friends of Eddie Coyle*, *Sorcerer*, and other terrific 1970s flicks.

On August 15, 2009, I was invited by the Royal York's head beekeeper and marketing boss Melanie Coates to join the annual bee harvest on the hotel's roof. The beehives are adjacent to the herb garden where Chefs David Garcelon and Ryan Gustafson often come for herbs and specialty vegetables for their kitchen (I don't think I've ever seen so many different varieties of tomatoes grown in a non-farm setting). I had never given beekeeping or honey production that much thought before her invitation, but when she asked me I was certainly intrigued, excited, and a little nervous.

I met Melanie and the team of professional beekeepers on the roof as they harvested honey from the hives. How the sweet stuff was extracted was something I knew nothing about. The beekeepers were decked from head to toe in white and wore helmets and netting over their faces. All pant legs and sleeve openings were either tucked in or closed off with tape.

The process began with tin pots filled with combustibles set alight, causing smoke to waft over the hives. This technique tricked the bees into thinking there was a fire and made them gorge themselves on honey, then get the hell out of the hives. When this part of the procedure was in full swing, thousands of bees buzzed around in a cloud. After the bees were gone, the honeycombs were extracted from the hives and gathered up to take below to the kitchen where the next step took place.

I watched in utter fascination, not just the method but the respect these beekeepers had for their little charges, admiration that moved into a kind of well-justified reverence as they described in loving detail what was going on in the hives and how it worked with a natural purity few of us notice anymore.

When I actually got stung on the neck by a bee and before I could panic, Chef Garcelon urged me to step inside away from the bees for a moment. He said that if I started freaking out and swatted at them I would make matters worse. I didn't blame the bee, of course. I was stupid enough to wear a spritz of cologne, having forgotten the directive not to do so around hordes of bees.

The next step in this honeybee odyssey took place in the kitchen on the convention floor of the Royal York. To call it a kitchen is like saying the *Titanic* was a boat. The Royal York's kitchen has endless canyons of fryers, ovens, counters, and sinks. The honey extraction was set up in the back corner of the cavernous kitchen, and what was remarkable about this part of the process was how wonderfully low-tech it was. Wax was gently sliced from the honeycombs, allowing the honey to ooze out. Then the honeycombs were placed in a hand-cranked metal centrifuge where gravity pulled the honey out, causing it to drip through a filter into a container.

Melanie urged me to take some of the honey-soaked wax from the pan and eat it in its most pristine state (or with a piece of Canadian cheddar also on hand). I did so, and what I tasted was divine. It was sweet, but naturally so. I joked with Melanie that I wasn't sure I had the words to describe how absolutely delicious this stuff was as it slid down my throat, other than to say it was what Mozart's music tasted like.

Another thing I observed was that while this was serious business for the professional beekeepers, it was also rich and rewarding fun. As the various steps were taken in the harvesting of the honey, everyone involved smiled. The bees had done their job magnificently; now their human partners were doing theirs.

When I left the kitchen once the harvesting was complete (and after grabbing another hunk of honey-soaked wax to chew on), I noticed something that seemed surreal. Amid the blur of organized commotion, cooks and chefs moving from here to there with sauce-spattered aprons, room service carts rolling around everywhere, sat a large round table elegantly decked out as if it were sitting in the middle of EPIC. People sat around the table enjoying what looked like a very fine meal. The best silverware and wineglasses were being used, and the talk around the table was quiet and respectful, even though the mammoth hotel kitchen was running on all cylinders around the diners. These people were there to sample the various aspects of the menu they were planning for a wedding or some other elegant gathering in the hotel. They were sampling the

food and service and were plotting their occasion on the spot
with the help of the Royal York's expert team of event planners.

Later that day, as I went back to my suite though the lobby,
I spotted people coming and going with tourist maps in hand,
heading either out to explore or returning from an outing.
Conventioneers were huddled together as they pored over
agendas and itineraries. I smiled. If they all knew what had
transpired on the roof and in the kitchen today, it would make
them appreciate the Royal York even more.

In March 2010 the Royal York was the headquarters and
ground zero for Canadian Music Week. The hotel was instantly
transformed from the controlled hustle and bustle of a luxury
hotel to the pandemonium, noise, and manic energy that results
when a building is filled to the brim with musicians, record label
people, and other assorted music industry freaks. The energy of
the place increased tenfold instantly. When I strolled through
the lobby or the cluttered mezzanine level where people had set
up displays, I saw piles of cards and flyers strewn everywhere
from bands trying to get industry professionals and music fans
alike to come to their shows during CMW. Bands with names
such as The Balconies and Versus the Nothing were in town,
and the air was electric. I could feel it crackle all around me as
I explored the hallways. Up in the suites every door I passed
had the sounds of parties or meetings going on. One evening
Melissa Auf der Maur, the ex-bassist in Courtney Love's band
Hole, stopped by during CMW. She asked me if I was "the
writer Christopher Heard." I said I was. Then she handed me an
advance copy of her new CD and asked if I'd listen to it. I said I
would, and did. It was fantastic!

Thursday morning of that Canadian Music Week had me off to the hotel swimming pool for my usual hour of laps. Although the Royal York buzzed loudly day and night, I was relatively sure there wouldn't be any music freaks in the pool at 7:00 a.m. I was wrong, though. Two other guys were in the pool area. One was swimming laps, while the other, a mountain of a man, seemed to be watching his companion in the water. I got into the pool and began my laps, as well. As I passed the fellow doing his own laps, there was something very familiar about him. Then I connected his face to a big poster outside the Imperial Room. He was Slash, the lead guitarist from Guns N' Roses. The big dude was his assistant/bodyguard. Slash was the headliner for an event that morning and was slated to do an interview in front of a packed room of musicians, reporters, and fans.

The next morning, Friday, I was down for my laps as usual. Slash and his eagle-eyed bodyguard were in the health club, with Slash running on the treadmill. After he finished exercising and I did my laps, we shared an elevator and chatted about the hotel. I told Slash that I lived in the Royal York, was actually conceived here, and was writing a book about hotel living. He smirked as he left the elevator, then said, "Man, I could tell you stories about hotel living, although they'd certainly change the tone of your book." About that I had no doubt.

One of the truly fascinating things about living in a hotel is that the surroundings always remain the same. In the case of the Royal York they haven't changed in 80-odd years, with the exception of the addition built in 1959, but the atmosphere constantly shifts depending on the kinds of people there at any given time. Earlier I described the ambience surrounding the invasion during Canadian Music Week, but that vibe was quite different a couple of days before when the Royal York was packed with prospectors and miners. For a week I had casual conversations with all kinds of swashbucklers and dry-gulchers who had come from Yukon Territory and other mountainous regions around the world. During that week, the one thing I was asked more than anything else was: "Where's the Brass Rail from here?" (The Brass Rail is a well-known, well-established Yonge Street institution in Toronto. Depending on your point of view, you can call it a gentlemen's club or simply what it is — a strip joint.)

One evening during that week I was sitting at the bar in the EPIC lounge chatting with a fellow whose business was platinum. As we talked and drank, he abruptly said, "I want you to check something out, son." (If he was five years older than I was, I'd be surprised.) He unsnapped his watch and handed it to me. Being a lover of nice watches, I was impressed by the piece. It was a platinum Rolex with a nice helping of diamonds glittering on its face. Like all luxury watches, it had weight to it, a detail I soaked up. The platinum man said, "That's $30,000 worth of watch you're holding there, boy."

I knew it was very valuable, and not knowing what else to say, simply asked, "Can I have it?"

He frowned, then grinned. "For a second there I thought you were serious."

"For a second there I was." Then I handed him back the watch.

Two groups I've grown quite accustomed to seeing are flight crews from British Airways and Air Emirates, both of whom use the Royal York as their regular stopover destination. There is a military precision to their arrival and departure. I always know the Air Emirates crew. The female flight attendants are gorgeous, and their uniforms are a sight to behold — gold and red, with thin kerchiefs wrapped around their heads, slightly covering quite the variety of faces. Air Emirates has a policy of employing a richly multicultural, multiracial mix of people. When the airline's crews gather in the hotel lobby, it is like watching a fashion show at the United Nations in which all the models are uniformly dressed.

The British Airways crews are friendly and try to make the best of their long hours and time zone challenges. One August I had a wonderful conversation in the hotel lobby with a delightful British Airways flight attendant — a beautiful young lady named Deirdre. She held my rapt attention as she told me that her five years as a British Airways flight attendant had given her a whole new perspective on time, space, and distance. Deirdre also provided me with a new way of looking at flight attendants and what their work entailed. As she headed to the bus taking her crew to the airport, she glanced over her shoulder at me, winked, and said that flight crews worked very hard but played even harder. I smiled at her comment without having the proper frame of reference to know what she meant. But my frame of reference expanded during the waning days of that August when an episode involving a visiting flight crew from a major European carrier enlightened me further.

On that especially sultry evening I was doing what had become my routine — writing all day, then after dinner a stroll to Harbourfront, then a stop by EPIC for a quick cognac and a scan of the room to see if there were any good stories floating about. While I was there two flight attendants came by for a glass of wine. I'll call them Gwen and Lucille. Both were in their mid- to late thirties and had been flight attendants for at least ten years each. As the wine flowed, we talked about the Royal York and other hotels we'd mutually visited, such as the Royal Windsor in Brussels and the Royal Pavilion in Barbados. One of the women, Gwen, became flirtier as her wine intake grew, and when it was discovered that all three of us shared a love of European soccer, the conversation got even more animated.

Once they'd downed two glasses of wine and I'd had two cognacs, I noticed that Gwen was getting a bit more touchy-feely with me. Her hand squeezed my arm or my thigh, and she leaned closer to me when making a point. Eventually, she inquired if I'd ever been with two women at the same time. I said that I hadn't. With a sly smile she then asked if I "fancied a go" with her and Lucille.

I smiled uncomfortably and looked at Lucille. She smiled and raised her eyebrows a few times. I told Gwen that I thought they were both equally sexy girls but that the offer was probably the wine talking.

She was relentless, though. "C'mon now. Don't tell me you've never thought about what it would be like with two little birds at the same time."

I told her that if I had it was certainly not all that frequently.

"C'mon, let's give it a go. It'll be a wonderfully fun way to pass the evening."

I really couldn't argue with her notion but that didn't change the fact that I wasn't going to comply no matter how tempting the mathematics were. The night ended with Gwen and Lucille ambling arm in arm toward the main elevators, while I headed to the east elevators. Later I ran into Lucille and Gwen on two other occasions, but there was no mention of that first encounter.

Sometime after that summer I had an even more blatant experience with sexuality, one that involved someone right across the hall from my room. A renewable energy convention was in town, and one of the conventioneers, a petite, athletic woman just north or south of 40, was in the suite directly across the hall from mine. I saw her in the gym on the treadmill in the mornings, shared pleasantries with her in the elevator, and had a brief chat when we waited for rides outside the front entrance of the hotel. Having seen so many people come and go, having had casual conversations with lots of fellow guests, there was nothing extraordinary, from my perspective, about anything I shared with this woman.

One night, however, as I was reading some magazines after writing all day I heard something being slipped under my door. I picked up the envelope, which had nothing written on it, and opened it. Inside was a card key with a sticky note on it. It read: "My last night in town." There was also a piece of paper in the envelope. I unfolded the paper, and to my astonishment there was a self-taken photo (hastily printed, no doubt, on a portable printer) of my neighbour naked on her bed in an utterly suggestive pose.

Oscar Wilde had pretty similar thoughts to mine on such occasions, especially when he had Lord Darlington in *Lady Windermere's Fan* say, "I can resist everything except temptation." But again there were a number of reasons why as flattering as this woman's overture was and as momentarily intoxicating as the whole notion seemed, I didn't make the trip across the hall that night. And do keep in mind that the vast majority of my days and nights as an author living in the Royal York aren't epic bouts of swinging from the chandeliers, waking up with a different woman each morning, and finding female underwear of unknown origin in my bathroom. Anything but, in fact.

When I'm working hard to fulfill a writing deadline, my days are rigidly routine — up early, down to the health club to swim laps in the pool, a perusal of the morning paper, a brief chat with Josh, write all morning, out for a walk and a bite of lunch, write for the afternoon, out for dinner, review the day's writing and outline what to work on the next day. After all that it's time for some relaxation — perhaps a sip or two of cognac before bed. That's my usual routine, but it's a schedule that needs to be stepped out of at regular intervals to preserve my version of sanity.

A cliché becomes a cliché in most cases because there are more than a few elements of truth to them. One of the naughtiest clichés that surrounds hotel living is the presence of call girls. I've been in many fine hotels in cities such as New York and Los Angeles and have easily spotted ladies of the evening drifting to and fro through the lobbies and lounges either conducting business or prowling for it. Twice in particular I witnessed the seeking of business, if not the actual conducting of it.

Such activity was so casually commonplace at the Four Seasons in Beverly Hills that whenever I found myself there with a fellow TV person or a producer, we went to the pool and sat on opposite sides by ourselves. Typically, we'd bet on who got propositioned first by one of the ladies of the night, with the winner owed lunch or dinner by the loser. On one occasion, within minutes, a girl came down from the cabana area in a tight, skimpy bikini. Strutting around the pool, she sized up the potential, then sat beside me. "So, like, where are you from?" she asked.

Having already won the lunch bet, my answer was: "So, like, I don't have 500 bucks on me."

At the Regency in New York City I saw producer Don Simpson (*Top Gun, Flashdance*), former partner of producer

Jerry Bruckheimer, come and go (before he died of a cocaine-induced heart attack), often with anywhere between two and four young women on his arms. One night I spotted him climbing out of a limo with one of his girls and a bottle of Tanqueray gin. Openly, for anyone to hear, he said, "Okay, let's see what five grand buys me."

One thing I can honestly say is that I've seen very little evidence of such goings-on at the Royal York. So *do* call girls turn up there? Of course, they do. There isn't a hotel or motel anywhere in the world where ladies of the night don't ply their trade, but at the Royal York such business isn't overtly evident. One hot September evening during the Toronto International Film Festival, though, I came upon two of the most obvious cases I've witnessed anywhere on the planet. To date it's the only time I've personally encountered the world's oldest profession within the Royal York's hallowed walls.

As I walked through the lobby toward the bank of east elevators and passed the entrance to EPIC, I noticed two garishly overdressed Russian women sizing up the place. You might wonder how I knew instantly that these women were Russian. Well, the lethal spike-heeled shoes they wore helped. The foot-wide gold belts with giant glittering Dolce & Gabbana buckles also tipped me off, not to mention the skintight jeans, blouses opened to solar plexuses displaying beach-ball-sized fake breasts with tans that actually looked as if they might be authentically earned. Of course, the fact that the ladies were speaking loudly in Russian to each other also confirmed their nationality.

It was pretty apparent that these two were on the prowl for business, so I decided to investigate the situation a bit further. Strolling past them a few times, I caught one, then the other's eye until finally earning a pair of "we might just have a fish hooked here" smiles. The bustier of the pair said, "Hi dere."

As soon as I said hello, the other lady asked, "You like par-tee?"

I replied that I was known to like a party or two here and there, then smiled and made it obvious I was checking out their goodies. They suggested we go into EPIC for a drink to talk first. I thought their story was worth a glass of wine or two, so we went inside and took a small table near the entrance. They ordered double vodkas and began asking questions about which bank I used, what kind of car I drove, what I did for a living. Clearly, these two were sex-for-hire fraudsters bent on screwing me, then really screwing me!

The really breasty one told me that if I wanted one or the other for the night it would cost "one thoe-sund doe-laars." And if I wanted both of them, it would be "one thoe-sund, five hune-ded, doe-laars." I figured what I'd already spent on their double vodkas was worth way more than what they were offer-ing. Still, the blatant nature of their play was astounding and fascinated me. I asked what I could expect for the fees. They both promised it would be something I'd never experienced before. Since I'd never been the victim of identity theft previ-ously, I had to agree they were likely telling me the truth about that. The truly breasty one then laid out what they had in store for me in graphic, bad 1970s porn terms. It ranged from the curiously titillating to the absurdly acrobatic to the downright ridiculous. Her partner in crime then semi-discreetly pro-duced a small video camera and told me that for an extra $300 we could make a "vee-deeo" of the goings-on.

When they were about to order another round of double vodkas on me, I decided I'd had enough. I told them there was one question they should have asked me first. Both looked at me quizzically. I smiled and said they should have asked, "Are you a cop?" Even under the inch and a half of makeup that looked as if it were applied by Clara the Clown, Master Face Painter, I saw the colour drain from their faces. Without another word they grabbed their bags and sashayed toward the nearby exit as fast as their stiletto heels could take them.

Briefly, I considered reporting the pair to security so they could be on the lookout for the confidence hookers, but the Russians were so transparent that I figured security didn't need my help identifying them. Likewise I was confident that no one staying at the Royal York would be gullible enough to fall for such obvious scammers. I never did see the Russians again, so perhaps I scared them off for good.

One of my passions in life is soccer. For many years I've followed the exploits of Real Madrid, the Galácticos and White Angels of European soccer. While I've read books and countless magazine articles about them and watched many of their La Liga and Champions League matches on television, I'd never seen them play live. But that was about to change, and I wouldn't have to travel very far at all.

One summer evening I was called by my Royal York friend Melanie Coates who asked if I would join her for a dinner in EPIC she was hosting for a group of European journalists in town and staying in the hotel to spread the word about the place in Spain, Switzerland, Belgium, and Sweden. Upon meeting the group in the lobby, I learned that two of the beautiful young women representing Spain were actually from Madrid and were also huge Galáctico fans. One of them regularly attended games at Santiago Bernabéu Stadium because her magazine had a box and often took guests or advertisers there. I told them I wanted to sit with them at dinner because we had a whole lot to talk about. All of this was occurring in the middle of the wildest times for Real Madrid. The team had just spent hundreds of millions of euros buying up every star player and sniper from around the world, including Brazilian ace Kaká, then the French star Karim Benzema. Only days before our dinner at the Royal York, Real Madrid paid a record-breaking sum for Portuguese superstar Cristiano Ronaldo.

As we chatted over dinner, one of the Spanish women said she had actually been at Santiago Bernabéu when Ronaldo was first introduced to his new fans. I sat in impressed silence as she described the scene for me. Eighty thousand people showed up to see Ronaldo come onto the field, be introduced, then strut around wearing his dazzling new white home uniform.

After a wonderful dinner, Chef Ryan Gustafson paid us a visit during which he explained the unique aspects of the menu for us, including herbs from the hotel's rooftop herb garden and fresh meat, produce, and seafood from nearby St. Lawrence Market. We then sat around and talked until well after the place closed. When the time to pack it in finally arrived and we left the restaurant, I continued a conversation with a Belgian journalist and didn't notice that directly behind me was my lovely Spanish writer friend who had earlier turned me green with envy with her tales of watching Real Madrid play. She stopped and bent to adjust a strap on her sandal. I looked ahead just as we collided. Instinctively, I reached out to prevent her from toppling over, but because of her position I found myself with one hand on her hip and the other on her soft, round derrière. We both laughed the moment off, and I apologized profusely for putting my hands on her in such a familiar manner. She said it was perfectly all right, that she would much rather have me grab her bottom than knock her on the head.

I've never spoken with or communicated with any of the dinner companions I met that evening, but every time I see a Real Madrid game on television I think of that Spanish journalist watching the game, too, at Santiago Bernabéu Stadium, stoked with the knowledge that I'd actually held one of the posteriors sitting there in my hands, the closest I've ever gotten to being a spectator myself.

But the story gets better, and I believe the magic of the Royal York was responsible for producing what happened next. A couple of days after the dinner with the European journalists I got a call from Jack Flynn at Adidas. He had heard me speaking about my love for Real Madrid on the radio and told me that not only was the team coming to Canada to play a friendly match with Toronto FC but Adidas was holding a private function with the players in the upper level of the Adidas store at Dundas Square. Would I like to meet the guys? Like a ten-year-old kid, I paced around the floor as I told Jack I most certainly did want to be on hand for the event.

As it turned out, I got to eat and drink with 12 Real Madrid players, who chatted with the guests, signed autographs, and posed for pictures. To this day under a sheet of glass on my coffee table in my suite at the Royal York I have a blow-up photo of me with the team — another magical moment!

Christmas at the Royal York is made all the more wonderful because the people who work in the hotel and the guests make it so. One day in late November 2009 the official lighting of the Christmas tree took place in the lobby, the cast of the musical *The Sound of Music* (then playing at the Princess of Wales Theatre) was on hand to sing carols, and the presentation of a donation to a local children's charity occurred. I was surprised at how emotional I found the proceedings. When the tree was lit and the carolling began, I actually choked up. The huge tree stood to the west of the main entrance while to the right was a giant gingerbread rendition of the hotel decked out with jelly beans and candy canes.

On the day of the tree lighting a table was set up and everyone stopping by was treated to eggnog. As the presentation of the donation to the children's charity happened, it was made even more special when a frequent guest, a wonderful man I've come to enjoy talking to in the health club on a regular basis (a fellow who was once the U.S. ambassador to Bermuda), stepped forward and said he would personally double what had been raised by the hotel staff. I realized at that ceremony that I hadn't given any thought to putting up decorations of my own in my suite. Of course, there was no need to, since all of the decorations in the hotel were essentially mine, too.

New Year's Eve is a night you expect the wheels to come off and things to take place that are odd even for a hotel. I certainly wasn't disappointed during my first New Year's Eve living at the Royal York. Around midnight I heard running in the hallway and yelling, not party shouting but security guard hollering. I poked my head out the door and saw a security guard chasing a man at full gallop. When I offered to help, the security man said, "Please, sir, get back inside and close the door. I have this under control." He then continued down the hallway after the man. I never did find out why the fellow was being chased or what happened to him when he was caught.

At about 1:30 a.m. something even stranger occurred that I look back on with a chuckle. There was a weak, uneven knock on my door. I peered through the peephole and spied a woman standing there. When I opened the door, the woman, pretty, slim, and in her mid-thirties, was dressed from the waist up in a cashmere turtleneck sweater. She wore a handsome watch and an elegant necklace, was done up in full makeup, and had her hair styled as if she'd attended a nice party or dinner. From the waist down she was wrapped in a towel and her feet were bare. Oh, and the woman was hammered.

When I told her she had the wrong room, she waved her card key at me and said, "I don't know what room is the right room. I can't remember the room I'm in. The numbers are funny here." She handed me the card key and asked what suite she was in. I told her there was no way to tell from the card. She started to cry, then moaned, "What am I going to do? I don't know where to go!"

I suggested she come in, we would call security, she could give them her name, and they would come up and escort her to her room. She entered, staggered over to my bed, threw the towel onto the floor, and revealed she was naked from the waist down. The woman then flopped heavily and awkwardly onto the bed. I tried to keep her awake, because without her name I couldn't do anything further for her. Patting her hand, I pleaded with her to stay awake and tell me her name. She slurred something, but I couldn't understand what it was, then she wailed, "Why can't I sleep? I want to sleep."

Shaking my head, I covered her with the towel, called downstairs, and explained everything to a security man. He told me he was well aware of the situation and would send another security guy already on the case to my room. While I waited the woman suddenly asked if I had anything to drink! I simply shook my head. She then mumbled that she wanted to take a shower before bed. I told her someone was on his way up to get her back to her room, so she should hang on. I also suggested that it might be wise to wait until she could stand on her own before trying a shower. When the security man arrived, I let him in. In his hand he had a purse, a pair of black slacks, a pair of high heels, and black panties.

"Are those hers?" I asked.

"Well, based on the other half of her outfit," he replied, "I'd say that's a good guess." He told me that the woman had taken the elevator up. When the doors opened, she had stepped into the ninth-floor foyer and must have thought she was already in her suite. She had taken off her shoes, slacks, and panties and left them in a heap under the long table in the foyer. After she realized she wasn't in her suite, she had likely dug out her key but couldn't remember the suite number, so with her key she had tried to open the first door she'd seen, disturbing the older gentleman in that suite. He had handed her a towel and told her to cover herself up, then had shut the door and called downstairs.

I told the security man to check the woman's purse for ID and then call down with the name. He said she hadn't authorized him to look inside her purse, so he was uncomfortable doing so. I told him I wasn't a hotel official and had no problem rifling through her purse. He laughed and gave me the purse. When I found a picture ID with her name on it, I gave it to the security man and he called down and got the number of the suite, which was at the other end of my hallway.

We got the woman to her feet amid a volley of slurred protests. I tied the towel around her waist as securely as I could and, assisted by the security man, helped her to the door. I asked him if he wanted me to help him get her to her room. He said he could take care of that but asked if I could follow him with her clothes and purse. Once we got the woman inside her suite, she flopped onto the bed with the towel still wrapped around her. I put her clothes and purse on the chair, and the security man placed the key on the desk in an obvious spot. Then we left, wishing each other a Happy New Year. Just another night of hotel living!

Unlike many hotels, the Royal York actually courts movie and television productions. Most big hotels also allow shows and films to be shot in their midst, but they're nervous about it since the production companies take over whatever space they've invaded and don't care much about what's going on around them. Their only focus is to get the work done, secure the necessary footage, and do it as quickly and as cost-efficiently as possible. About ten years ago Kolene Elliott, a beautiful, bright, engaging, friendly young woman, literally created a position for herself at the Royal York. She scoured the planet to lure film and TV productions to the Royal York as their location. At first Kolene's position was experimental, but a decade and 250 or so productions later, she is a star in her own right.

Because a hotel must keep the needs and comforts of guests as a first priority, it is always dicey when a big movie production rolls in and uses the interior and sometimes the exterior of the hotel as a location. They need to block access to their sets, which means guests can't roam freely in the areas of the hotel the production company has taken over. "That was and is always a big concern," says Kolene. "But what we tried to establish early on and continue to do is make the experience part of the guest's experience, include the guests in the excitement by letting them feel that not only are they staying in this big grand old hotel but there is also a big Hollywood movie being shot here, as well, and the stars and the action are a unique and special part of their stay."

Over the years the Royal York has played host to many important and not so significant films. Producers I've spoken to on Royal York sets have cited reasons for being there that included Kolene's terrific selling job, the spaciousness of the hotel, and the great interiors and exterior that can be used for almost every imaginable era. Ron Howard and Russell Crowe employed the exterior and interiors of the Royal York for their Depression-era *Cinderella Man*. The inside and outside of the hotel found their way into *Hollywoodland*, a movie set in the 1950s and starring Ben Affleck. The Emmy-winning Drew Barrymore HBO movie *Grey Gardens* also found a home in the Royal York, while Jackie Chan utilized the hotel for his contemporary action comedy *The Tuxedo* in which many levels of the roof saw action with spectacular stunts.

In the late winter of 2010, *RED*, one of the largest, most complicated productions ever shot at the Royal York, rolled into town. The film is an action-adventure flick based on a noir-ish graphic novel of the same name. The director of the film is German filmmaker Robert Schwentke, who also helmed *The Time Traveler's Wife*. *RED* stars Bruce Willis as an aging, retired black ops commando who is suddenly stalked by an assassin. To protect himself he reassembles his old commando unit long enough for him to figure out why he is being targeted. Also in the film are Morgan Freeman, Mary-Louise Parker, John Malkovich, and Helen Mirren.

Shooting a major Hollywood film like *RED* is akin to waging a small war. Precise logistical plans have to be made, and when the equipment and stars arrive, everything has to be ready to go. In today's Hollywood, spending $300,000 to $500,000 daily on location isn't unheard of. So any day a production company can't keep to its schedule means considerable added expense. On a production the size of *RED*, a team of producers, production managers, art directors, and set designers arrive weeks in advance to work with Kolene and her people to ensure the machine is fully tuned when the main army hits the hotel.

One of the executive producers of *RED* is Jake Myers, a friendly, always somewhat physically drained guy who explained to me that he had shot a number of movies in the Royal York, but never one that huge. "This is a big one, and we're here because we couldn't get the kind of support, co-operation, and physical space we need in any other hotel. We looked at other places, but because I had shot here before and knew Kolene, I knew we'd eventually end up shooting here."

I asked Myers if he was concerned during a big hotel shoot about the guests in the hotel. "Of course, we think about doing our jobs first, but we want to be respectful and maintain a good positive working relationship with Kolene and the hotel people, so we do everything we can to make sure the guests aren't put out or disturbed when we're shooting. But sometimes, as in the case of this film, that's unavoidable."

What Myers was referring to were two things: the need to close Front Street and shut down the entrance of the hotel to the public so exterior scenes could be filmed, and the inevitability of loud gunfire and explosions in certain locations such as the hotel's kitchen. One morning I headed to the pool for my usual laps. On this occasion, though, a sign outside the steps leading into the health club read: DEAR GUESTS, DO NOT BE ALARMED BY THE SOUNDS OF LOUD EXPLOSIONS AND THE SOUNDS OF LOUD AND PROLONGED GUNFIRE. AN ACTION MOVIE IS BEING FILMED IN THE HOTEL. While I never heard the gunfire, health club attendant Josh Stone and I did hear test gunfire. The stunt guys blasted away for as long as required, then went to the health club and the lobby and asked about the level of noise heard in those places. It was pretty loud, but just another one of the eccentricities that comes with living in a hotel.

I often hung out at various hotel locations for *RED* and talked to the cast and crew. An actor friend of mine, Tarik Hassan, was playing a small role in the film, so we chatted about the shoot or met for a cognac during long breaks. It was funny because when we met in EPIC he left the set wearing a tuxedo, while I was in worn jeans and a T-shirt. Guests coming into EPIC looked at him as if he were James Bond.

During the filming of a scene involving a political dinner, the ballroom on C Floor was used as a location, the Imperial Room became a holding area for cast members and extras, and the Upper Canada Room, high in the hotel, served as a makeup and wardrobe area. On C Floor huge black curtains were hung to close in the set, not for secrecy (though there was an element of that) but to keep the commotion and noise to a minimum.

When *RED*'s production company took over the street for exterior shots, keeping noise down wasn't possible. Several tons of equipment rolled in, including trucks, cranes, scaffolding, huge lights, dolly tracks, and miles and miles of snaking cables. On one particular night Front Street was decked out in Christmas lights, and the facade of the Royal York was disguised as a U.S.-based Fairmont hotel, with all the flags changed and police cars with U.S. city markings on display.

It was awfully chilly that night, so I didn't linger on the set much, though I was there long enough to chat briefly with Helen Mirren. Dame Helen is the nicest, smartest, most unpretentious movie star I've ever encountered. That evening she sat in the back seat of a black Bentley, eating a Wendy's double burger most enthusiastically. I told her that Queen Elizabeth II stayed in the Royal York when she was in Toronto.

"Yes, I saw the pictures in the mezzanine," Dame Helen said. "Have you ever seen her?"

At the time I hadn't, so I said, "No, you're actually the closest I've gotten so far." (Mirren plays Queen Elizabeth II in *The Queen* and won many well-deserved awards for her acting.) I told Dame Helen that I lived in the Royal York and that I was literally conceived there, something I always have an urge to tell everybody.

She smiled. "Right then. We'll try not to make too much of a mess of your home."

On just one occasion the shooting of *RED* proved intrusive, and that was something minor. Outside and several floors below my suite window is a roof. Because the production company was filming scenes in an alley below that roof, the lighting guys had to build an enormous contraption that involved walkways, railings, and safety cables to support the three mammoth lights rigged to illuminate the alley. During the couple of days it took to erect the lighting rig on the roof, I glanced down every now and then to check the progress. Each time I did I was amazed at how much more gear had been added, but I thought nothing more about it. I had been on hundreds of movie sets, so I'd witnessed this sort of thing before. That night, though, around 1:00 a.m., I woke up suddenly. For a moment I thought I had either slept in until high noon the next morning or that a UFO was hovering outside my window. My whole suite was bathed in white light. Peering out the window, I saw the three huge lights fired up and an action scene in progress involving stuntmen running around in the alley below. I watched the scenes for a while, then went back to sleep. When I woke up again at 6:00 a.m., it was darker in the room than it had been at 1:00 a.m. The sequences had been completed, and it was time to move on to the next scene.

A surrealistic air reigns at the Royal York when movies are shot there. Take August 16, 2010, for example. For me the day started like most other ones — a visit to the health club, then out for breakfast with Rhonda, my lady friend. But on this day something was different. As we passed through the lobby, the area leading to the Imperial Room was roped off. Clearly, a film scene was in progress. The surrealism was supplied by the flags with the U.S. presidential seal on them flanking the entrance to the Imperial Room where a "state dinner" was being shot. Greg Kinnear and Katie Holmes were in their finest formal wear playing President John F. Kennedy and First Lady Jackie. They were shooting the television miniseries *The Kennedys*, and it was downright eerie to see Kinnear as Kennedy in the Imperial Room. Later I asked Kinnear, whom I'd met and interviewed three times previously, about filming in the Royal York.

"I have to say it helped," said Kinnear. "I mean, it's still work. You still have to concentrate to stay in your character and in that character's time and space, but when you're in a place that comfortably and naturally reflects that time and space, it's much easier to slip into it. You don't have to expend energy on that so you can refocus that saved energy on the specifics of your performance."

Whenever my daughter, Isabelle, visits at the Royal York, she becomes a real-life Eloise as she races up and down the wide mezzanine floor and twirls and giggles in the lobby while gazing up at the ornate woodwork and gleaming chandeliers. It's wonderful to watch the imagination of a curious little girl as she lets her playfulness run rampant. Every time we approach the hotel from the outside, she always looks up and asks if this is the kind of place where princesses live.

One afternoon we played in the halls and stairwells. It was raining outside, so we had to stay indoors and create a game that allowed us to lose ourselves completely in a fantasy world of our own making. At the time I was in the middle of a difficult publicity campaign for my book on Britney Spears. I had to get up at 4:30 every morning, sit in front of my computer, appear live on television shows in Europe and around North America via Skype, and answer endless questions. So a day of playing with my little beauty was just what the psychiatrist ordered!

The endlessly long hallways of the hotel fascinate Isabelle, and that day as we walked along them, she wanted to know what was on the other side of the fire doors. I told her we should take a look. As we peered at the old fire stairs, Isabelle said they reminded her of a dungeon in a giant's castle. So we went with that, whispering that we had to be quiet as we climbed the stairs to the next floor or risk waking the giant. Gingerly opening the fire door on the floor above, we peeked to make sure the coast was clear. Our adventure evolved rapidly as we ventured down the hallway to the fire door at the opposite end.

Isabelle spied a few discarded room service trays on the floor about halfway down the hall. She asked me what they were, and I explained that they carried the giant's food. Isabelle said we should grab his food as we passed so he would be hungry and have to leave to find something else to eat. Our mission identified, we inched along the hall, pressing against the wall. When we reached the trays, we snatched some used miniature ketchup bottles and jam jars, then scurried off as if a giant were pursuing us.

Stifling squeals of delight as her bare feet padded across the carpet, Isabelle made it to the opposite fire door and the cool safety of the dungeon, with me close behind. Heading up to the next floor, we glanced out. Again there was an abandoned room service tray halfway down the hall, but there was also a maid's cart. Isabelle asked me what that was. I told her it belonged to the giant's helper, so we had to be very careful when we passed it.

Ever so slowly we crept toward the tray. This time we scooped up some bread sticks and a couple of peanut butter containers, then took off to the other end of the hall. As we skirted the cart, a maid emerged from a room. Isabelle screamed, "It's the giant's helper! Run!"

The maid jumped and yelped as Isabelle and I bolted for our lives.

We continued playing the game for a couple of more hours, then returned to my suite to dump the loot we'd copped off the giant along the way. The couch in my suite took on the appearance of a garbage can. Soon it was time for Isabelle to return home with her mother. Down in the lobby, one of the hotel reception people stopped by to say hello. The woman shook Isabelle's hand and asked if she'd had a fun day. Isabelle waved her arms enthusiastically and replied, "We stole stuff!"

The hotel lady shot me a curious look.

"We had to," I said. "How else were we going to get the giant to leave?"

On another summer afternoon Isabelle and I played in my suite. I had asked my daughter if she wanted to go to Harbourfront to see the ducks, swans, and boats, but she said she was tired and wanted to draw pictures, then inflate a couple of balloons and play with them for a while. As we lay in bed on our backs, I blew up two oblong balloons and tossed them at the ceiling so Isabelle and I could catch them when they floated down. The bedroom window was open about eight inches, and a light breeze rippled in, gently swaying the curtains. I took Isabelle's balloon and pretended to shoot it toward the open window.

"No, Daddy, no!" she pleaded.

I did this a few times, then actually pushed the balloon toward the window, never expecting it to squeeze through the narrow gap and drift slowly to the roof below.

Isabelle stared at me in shock. "You threw my balloon out the window!"

I felt absolutely horrible seeing her confused little face. Hugging her, I told her I was very sorry and she could have my balloon. She said she didn't want my balloon; she wanted hers. Needless to say, we were shortly out the door and on our way to the Disney Store where I had serious amends to make.

In the long hallway to the main bank of elevators, we saw two maid's carts in front of rooms. Isabelle made a point of telling the maids, "Daddy threw my balloon right out the window!" When we got to the elevator and it arrived, we climbed on with a group of people from England. Again Isabelle ratted me out to anyone who would listen.

One of the British women turned to me and asked, "Did you really toss her balloon out the window?"

I said that I had but certainly not on purpose.

She then demanded, "How do you throw a little girl's balloon out the window by accident?"

I told the British woman we were on our way to the toy store to make the situation right.

The British woman patted Isabelle on the head. "You make sure he buys you something nice for throwing your balloon out the window."

When we got out of the elevator and headed to the east doors, Isabelle took my hand. "It's okay, Daddy. I forgive you."

$$\sim \quad \sim \quad \sim$$

Earth Hour is staged on the last Saturday in March between 8:30 and 9:30 p.m. As I've mentioned previously, the Royal York has a deep commitment to green issues. For Earth Hour the Royal York dims all the lights in the hotel and encourages guests to turn out their room lights during that time, as well. During Earth Hour in 2010, I hung out with Josh Stone. The swimming pool that night was an enchanted sight. The pool and hot tub area were ringed with a hundred little candles, giving the space an ethereal glow. More people than usual drifted into the pool area to be a part of the quiet energy radiating there. No one was actually swimming. Instead they floated around in a haze of dreamy relaxation. Guests from Japan, Germany, and the United States came by and uttered "Wow!" no matter what their native language actually was.

The lobby of the Royal York during Earth Hour in 2010 was a gasp-inducing vision when I first witnessed it. It was almost as if I'd stepped into a dream taking place in the 1930s. Were it not for the glow of computer screens at the reception desk, I would have thought I was strolling through the lobby in the days shortly after the hotel originally opened. The Library Bar, which the Royal York's management dims every weekend of the year as part of an ongoing regular commitment to Earth Hour, hummed with happy activity as people took pleasure in the novelty of unwinding without electricity. Sure, there was the odd killjoy who couldn't exist for an hour without resorting to his or her BlackBerry or iPhone, but most people, myself included, embraced the occasion with enthusiasm.

When it comes to the swimming pool at the Royal York, I've seen things that would make the most open-minded person shake his or her head. The pool is about 50 feet long, but not very deep at either end. It isn't an Olympic pool; it's for relaxation and/or swimming laps for exercise. Signs on every column warn people that diving is prohibited, since the water isn't deep enough for that kind of activity, yet I've lost count of the number of folks I've seen dive headfirst into the pool. Luckily, I haven't seen any fatalities yet.

Two diving incidents stand out in particular. The first involved a man who was about six foot seven and 270 pounds. He came in with a woman and was clearly trying to show her what an all-round wacky guy he was. This loud, boisterous bozo first embarrassed his lady friend by loudly slapping her derrière when she bent to adjust the lounge chair, then the classless oaf strutted over to the pool and readied himself to dive in headfirst.

I locked eyes with Will, the pool attendant that morning, and flicked my head toward the moron. Will saw what was happening and started to move in the direction of the miscreant, but he was too late. The fool threw himself into the water, and though he didn't hit his head on the bottom, he certainly scraped his chest and protruding gut. When the idiot stood in the water, we could all see angry red welts on his body. Then he proceeded to swim as noisily and with as much splashing as he could. I felt bad for his lady friend. She smiled uncomfortably every time the goof shot her a "Look at me, look at me" glance.

The other memorable "diving" occasion happened when a man north of 300 pounds entered the pool area and got ready to swim. I was at the east end in a chair reading a newspaper after doing my laps. The man waddled to the edge of the pool and flung himself in. When his girth hit the water, it caused such a displacement that a tsunami-like wave washed over the end of the pool. The man swam with broad strokes, setting off a constant swirl of choppy waves. I thought about getting back into the water for another workout, but swimming with this character would have been like taking a dip in the surf at Maui during a tropical depression.

When it comes to nudity, the pool at the Royal York has afforded me with more unintentional glimpses of body parts than I can count. Most are accidental, some occur due to amorous couples being unable to restrain themselves even for a brief swim, and a few are the result of cultural differences, since guests from some parts of Europe, Scandinavia, for instance, aren't weighed down by the hang-ups and repressed notions toward nudity largely prevalent in North America.

One of the cutest accidental unveilings I've observed in the Royal York's pool transpired when a woman took a dip with her daughter, who looked about six years old. They were having fun swimming underwater and racing, then the mother said she wanted to get out of the pool for a while. The little girl protested and hugged the mother to keep her in the pool. The mother insisted but said the little girl could remain for a while longer if she wanted. When the mother headed for the ladder and climbed the first rung, the little girl lunged at her and cried, "Stay in, Mommy, stay in!" Then she grabbed the mother's bathing suit bottom with the intention of pulling her back into the pool. What she managed to do instead was tug the mother's bathing suit bottom over her hips and just above her knees. The mother froze for a second, then squealed and leaped back into the pool to re-dress herself. Her daughter giggled and splashed — mission accomplished.

On another occasion four Norwegian woman, ranging in age from early twenties to about forty, were in the pool very early one morning. They were playing a game that involved sneaking up behind one another to pull their bikini tops off. I was swimming laps during this game, while other people in the pool area watched the spectacle of exposed breasts from the sidelines. An older gentleman sitting at the side of the pool with a newspaper seemed to get a lot of calls on his smart phone during the game. Every time I glanced at him he had the phone in his hand and was pointing it at the frolicking Scandinavians.

One Sunday morning I came down for a swim to find a young couple just entering the pool area. We said hello, and they told me they'd met at a wedding in the hotel the previous night and had "hooked up." Now weddings are notorious for that sort of thing, but I wasn't sure why these two needed to tell a perfect stranger about it.

Instead of going into the pool the couple headed over to the hot tub, so I slipped into the water to do my laps and dismissed them from my mind. But not for long. About a half-hour into my swim I heard a groan explode from the hot tub. I looked over and saw the woman straddling the man, her arms wrapped around his neck, her eyes shut tight, and her face in a grimace. She was bouncing up and down on his lap. I swam closer to the wall to block my view, not wanting to intrude on their very public private moment.

One of my most unforgettable pool experiences had nothing to do with sex or nudity. A convention of African-American engineers was taking place at the Royal York, and I found myself sharing the pool with at least 20 of the conventioneers on a Saturday morning. The spirited conversations I had with my pool mates covered everything from President Obama and Canadian health care to sports and the war in Iraq (a few of the men by the pool had done service there). Eventually, a man from Illinois asked me if I could keep an eye on his young daughter in the pool while he went for a sauna. I told him that would be no problem and that I had a little girl of my own. Then I gave some of the other engineers a brief history of the hotel and explained to them that they were in one of Canada's special places. As the engineers started drifting out of the pool area, an old guy from Indiana slapped me on the back and said, "It was nice meeting you, man. You're the blackest white guy I ever met." I took that as a compliment and marvelled at the couple of hours we'd spent together in and out of the pool.

That was hotel living at its best: a communal sharing of space and time in a comfortable place where the luxury and relaxation bring out the best in people who will likely never see one another again.

I had lived in the Royal York for more than a year before I was exposed to a real-life version of a cliché about hotels that pops up in movies and television programs all the time: the rhythmic thumping of vigorous sexual activity resounding through a neighbouring guest's wall.

On a warm and lovely late May day, Rhonda and I went for a long walk in the sunshine and stopped for lunch at a Thai restaurant. After that she headed home because she had an early day at work the next morning, while I returned to the Royal York to make notes and relax with the Lakers/Phoenix NBA playoff game. I was on the couch with my laptop on my knees trading email messages with my publisher when I heard what sounded like a protracted female groan. It distracted me for a moment, then I returned to what I was doing. Next I heard a thump on the wall. Because the game was on the television, I couldn't tell where the noise was coming from. I hit the mute on the remote, and the racket became quite distinct. It was coming through the wall directly over my left shoulder. There was another thump, then a womanly groan, then a thump, then another groan. So it finally dawned on me what was happening.

I smiled and shook my head, then turned up the TV so the couple could enjoy their fun without an accidental eavesdropper. It seemed, though, that as I raised the volume on the TV, they, too, upped the noise level of their activity. Now I wasn't just hearing thumping; there were breathy female cries of "Please don't stop!" and "Oh, yes, yes!"

Although I'm far from being a prude, I was starting to get a little irritated, even more so when the woman screeched, "You feel *soooo* huge inside me!" That was it. I had no choice now. Quickly, I jumped up, grabbed an ice bucket, rushed next door, and knocked loudly. Then I rapped a second time. Finally, the door opened, revealing a guy in his mid-fifties. He looked like a used car salesman. His face was red, he was breathing funny, and he had a Royal York robe hastily thrown on.

"Do you know where the ice machine is on this floor?" I asked.

He stared at me, then said he thought it was down the hall to the right but wasn't certain.

I apologized for bothering him and asked, "Brother, could you turn your TV down? I can hear the movie you're watching loud and clear through my wall."

Sheepishly, he nodded and closed the door.

As I walked back to my suite, I was wracked with guilt and kept thinking, *How would you feel if someone interrupted at probably the single worst time to interrupt a guy?* Back inside my room, I was amazed and then strangely relieved when I heard the couple take up where they had left off, minus the wall thumping, though. I figured they had either relocated to somewhere else in the room or simply changed the physical dynamic. This time I decided to go with the flow and let them enjoy their fun.

Not long after the above incident I participated in a delightful Royal York affair organized by Melanie Coates. The event was the inaugural Queen Victoria Look-Alike Contest. I was asked to be a celebrity judge for the competition, a task that turned out to be more complicated and stressful than I originally imagined. The contest took place in the open area west of the hotel lobby in front of the Imperial Room and the Library Bar. A runway for the contestants, a dais for the moderator, chairs for the audience, and a table for the judges were set up. My fellow judges included Melanie and my journalist pal, Shinan Govani, from the *National Post*. The event was co-sponsored by Victoria Gin (for somewhat obvious reasons), a British Columbia family-run distiller. I'm not a gin guy — cognac is my drink of choice — but I must admit that sipping the sponsor's variety was a pleasure. The host(ess) for the extravaganza was a drag queen named Miss Conception, who had a passing resemblance to Queen Victoria in her, or his, own right.

Seven young women vied for the crown. They were a varied, spirited bunch. Some were there for laughs and the free bottle of Victoria Gin everyone received. Others had clearly come to compete rather than merely ham it up. One woman in particular had researched Victoria's diaries; her presentation was a reading of some of the quirkier entries, which she delivered impeccably in period dress. Another older contestant was dressed appropriately, as well. She opted for re-enacting one of the many assassination attempts made on Victoria during her reign. Yet another charming contestant had discovered that Victoria liked to paint in her free moments, so that mock monarch sat demurely at an easel and painted a picture while dressed as the young queen. When she finished, she presented the painting of a Union Jack to the judges.

Our job as judges was to decide not only which contestant resembled Victoria the most, but how well they did their research and how good they were at balancing a glass of gin while walking down the runway regally. So as each contestant did what was asked of her by the moderator, we judges had to make notes and evaluate them, then gather in the Imperial Room to discuss and compare our findings. I was then nominated as the spokesperson. My duty was to take the microphone and compliment the ladies on at least one aspect of what they brought to the event.

After a brief, highly dramatic pause, I announced that the winner was the contestant who had interpreted Victoria as Mel Brooks would have depicted her. She respected the queen but was hysterically funny while doing so. Her presentation involved another aspect of the real Victoria's life: the British monarch's fascination with photography. So the contestant posed for a series of photos for the royal photographer — Victoria as gleeful, as heartbroken, playing with her dogs, and deep in thought. Every pose had displayed the same dour expression no matter what mood was being described. For her efforts she won a weekend in the Royal York's Royal Suite and breakfast in bed.

Exploring the hallways, conference rooms, and ballrooms of the Royal York is one of my favourite things to do, especially when they're completely empty and quiet. I like to inhabit the spaces and feel them without business meetings and parties going on. Being in the Imperial Room, for instance, when it's vacant makes that hallowed place seem even grander. When I wander around the hotel during the daytime, however, I'm often asked about the famous people I've encountered, given the fact that I do a lot of television and radio and write books on celebrities. After word got out that I was living in the Royal York, the questions shifted to a mix of queries about celebrities and about what it was like to live in a hotel.

A librarian, a true vanishing breed, recognized me one morning in the health club and asked if I was "that writer guy who lives in the hotel." When I told her I was, she said she knew I'd written a book while living in the Royal York and was working on another about the hotel-living experience, based on my mentioning the fact on several radio and television shows. She then asked if the act of writing had changed for me since living in the hotel. Upon reflecting on that, it dawned on me that I'd been on a strictly disciplined, rarely changing routine for months during the writing of my book on Kiefer Sutherland, a book on Britney Spears, and the beginning of *The Suite Life*. In more than a dozen years as a published author I'd never been as productive. When the librarian asked me what I attributed that to, it occurred to me that I'd become the hotel-living author I'd always imagined being — a sort of Ernest Hemingway or Cornell Woolrich.

I told her that for a writer, or any artist for that matter, living in a hotel removes all the minutiae from daily life. Making beds, taking out trash, doing laundry, all these small chores are eliminated from daily routine, leaving uncluttered time to focus attention on craft. Of course, for that to succeed discipline is needed, as well. A lot of people when given the opportunity to do nothing at all will do just that, but in my case the theory held and I was able to research and write two books with a velocity that was new to me.

Since the librarian and I were in the pool area, I explained that I always included health attendant Josh Stone in my pre-writing regimen by bouncing ideas off him so I could hear how they sounded, which was an important and highly valued part of my workday. I gave my new librarian friend a detailed rundown of my daily work because she was someone who understood what I did. In doing that I started to understand even more the connection between being a writer and the pull of hotel living.

Previously in this book I've mentioned elements of my daily life in the hotel. The day always begins with laps in the Royal York pool and a chat with health attendant Josh Stone, then a shower and out for a Tim Hortons coffee and a sausage breakfast sandwich on a homestyle biscuit. After that it's back to my laptop for a few hours of writing. Around noon I break for a walk and lunch, which often consists of beefy five-layer burritos. When that's done, I resume writing in my room until I stop for supper and another walk. Then it's back to work to go over what I've written that day and a possible conversation or email exchange with an editor on whatever problem has arisen. Relaxation follows, usually in the form of another walk if weather permits, a movie perhaps with Rhonda, and later a glass of cognac. Other times I might meet a friend in the Library Bar for a drink, or if I'm writing to a tight deadline, hit the computer again.

While I was toiling on various projects during that first long while in the Royal York, my work and pleasure routine continued without interruption until Prime Minister Stephen Harper and company arrived in Toronto in June 2010 for the madness of the G20 Summit. Harper and his court of fools decided the epicentre of that global idiocy would be the Royal York Hotel.

Actually, the first salvo of lunacy was fired in late March 2010 when Melanie Coates told me the G20 Summit would take over the hotel in a few months. She said the meetings would take place at the convention centre a couple of blocks west of the hotel and would last only two days. As we all learned later, the security tab for the whole affair (including the G8 Summit in the Muskoka region north of Toronto) ballooned to more than $1.5 billion to pay for draconian measures that transformed the Royal York and a good deal of the downtown core of the city into an ugly, fenced-in, armed encampment.

Melanie said I might have to leave the Royal York for a few days because the hotel would literally be taken over by the economic carnival. No guests would be allowed in the Royal York for the entire week leading up to the G20 Summit, only delegates, police, and employees. However, as it turned out, the people at the Royal York went to bat for me, and I was allowed to remain in my home during the summit. Still, I had to undergo an RCMP security clearance, as did everyone who had the temerity to live or work in Harper's temporary playground.

As the summit approached, high, ugly metal fences were erected around the Royal York, the convention centre, and the nearby Westin Harbour Castle Hotel, where President Barack

My security card for the G20 Summit was a necessary evil.

Obama would be based. Then it was time for me to undergo the scrutiny of the security clearance itself. I filled out a form that identified me as needing authorization to move around the "Red Zone" and to be inside the Royal York. After the form was completed, I visited a nearby bank tower for a chat with the Royal Canadian Mounted Police and to be photographed for the pass everyone had to wear around their necks at all times while inside the Royal York and carry concealed when outside the hotel. I was told the latter was necessary because "anarchists" would love to get their hands on a pass.

Anxiety levels increased dramatically as the week of the summit approached. Employees worried about how to behave, what they couldn't do, and where they couldn't go during the lockdown. When June 21 arrived, the security noose tightened around all our necks. Police in their thousands began arriving in hordes from across the country. Before the craziness ended almost ten times as many cops were inside the fence than Canada had troops fighting in Afghanistan, an overkill that was strangely surreal, terribly frightening, and very un-Canadian.

Initially, the police inside the fence weren't tense. In fact, there was almost air of a police convention in those early days. I saw a young policewoman from the Northwest Territories pose for pictures with RCMP tactical response guys and Toronto cops. The atmosphere was "let's all make the best of this strange scene."

One evening I brought Rhonda down to see the army of cops and the fences. She wasn't allowed inside the Royal York, of course, but we strolled around the Red Zone and shared pleasantries with RCMP officers guarding the Royal York and Calgary city police protecting King Street. In the mornings in the hotel's health club everything seemed different. Now my companions in the pool area were muscular tactical response cops, while their armoured brethren patrolled the halls and checked things out inch by inch.

Security was exceptionally tight. I had to show my security card to police to get inside the fence around the Red Zone (now nicknamed the Dirty Zone), then again to earn entrance to a second layer of fencing, then once more to enter the hotel itself. My security card was electronically scanned, and the picture that came up on a screen had to match the photo on the card or trouble would result. Once the card was verified, I had to empty my pockets and pass through a metal detector.

Every time I left the Royal York and returned, the rules of what could be brought into the hotel appeared to change. One moment I could bring in bottles, the next I couldn't. One hour I could bring in food, a little later I couldn't. Then I could bring in food again, but it had to be X-rayed. I soon got into the habit of checking with an RCMP officer in the hotel before leaving each morning to find out what the rules of the day were. Often he smiled and shrugged. He had no idea, either. As bizarre as this deranged situation was for me, it was even worse for the Royal York's employees. They were under such tight restrictions that once they swiped their time cards in the morning they weren't allowed to leave the hotel until they checked out at the end of the workday.

One morning I was at my desk writing and heard a knock. I assumed it was a maid, but when I opened the door I was startled by the sight of two RCMP bomb squad dudes and a bomb-sniffing German shepherd. "Good morning," one of the Mounties said. "Would you mind if we came in and checked your suite for explosives and bomb-making materials?"

I stared at them for a moment, then finally said, "Sure, come in. No bomb-making materials or explosives in here. Cognac, yes, explosives, no." The three of us stood there for a few seconds, then I said, "I've never been checked for bombs before. Do I stay here or go out or what?"

"Why don't you step out with me and let my partner and our dog do their thing?" the older bomb squad officer suggested.

So I went out and let the other officer and the dog, who I was told was named Sherlock, give my suite the once-over. The Mountie with me in the hall knew who I was. He asked me about living in a hotel and what the next book I was doing was about. Then Sherlock and the other officer came out, I was thanked for my co-operation, and they left.

Later that day I was back at work at my desk when I heard another knock. Opening the door, I saw four more heavily armed tactical guys standing there.

"Hey, man, you mind if we give your suite a bit of a search?" one of them asked.

I stepped out and told the lead cop, "The bomb guys checked the suite out this morning already."

"We're not bomb guys," one of the cops said.

These guys went through my suite inch by inch, scrutinizing the closet, drawers, even the door frames. Then one of them called out to me in the hallway, "Hey, man, can we have a shot of your cognac?"

I looked in the doorway and told them they could but only if I could join them. The oddity continued.

At one point my situation changed temporarily during those days. Melanie told me a problem was brewing because of my unique circumstances. One of the delegations and G20 leaders were staying on my floor, and since the Royal York had been completely taken over by the summit, nothing in terms of indulgences and special treatment were denied the visiting dignitaries or international protected persons (IPPs), as the cops called them. Apparently, international protocol dictated that a mere commoner such as myself wasn't allowed on the same floor as a foreign leader. I was certainly okay with that. I was willing to do whatever it took for everyone in the Royal York to get through Harper's madness as easily as possible.

It was first suggested that I might have to spend the weekend in another suite in another part of the hotel, leaving all my stuff behind. I was fine with that. Then it was decided I would have to pack up and move out of my suite entirely to another room, then move everything back after the party was over. Again I was more than willing to do what was required. All of us in the Royal York family were in the same boat. We were all sealed in like mixed nuts in a can. So that Friday morning I packed all my stuff and moved to a much smaller room. It was that day that things really started to go off the rails.

I had decided to get out of the Red Zone and head north. My friend, the filmmaker and Antarctica explorer Mark Terry, offered me his tickets to the Toronto FC/Los Angeles Galaxy soccer match being played in Toronto that Saturday evening. I stopped by his office for a chat and to pick up the tickets, then went next door to a restaurant that had a giant TV showing the World Cup game between my favourite team, Spain, and Chile. Relaxing for the afternoon, I had a big plate of spaghetti and meatballs and watched Spain move on to the next round of the tournament in South Africa.

As I headed home after the game, I noticed a commotion on Yonge Street below Wellesley. The street seemed to be closed, then I spotted a line of at least 30 unmarked vans with heavily armed, black-armoured riot cops hastily climbing out. They were loading tear gas guns and checking their arsenals. Some were donning black balaclavas. It was an exciting and disturbing sight, another slide down a rung of the ladder of weirdness surrounding all of us.

While Stephen Harper was posing for pictures with his G8 fat cat pals up north, his armies were turning Toronto into an urban combat zone. As I followed the unending rows of cops arming themselves to the teeth, I passed many stunned civilians. Walking south on Yonge, I spied riot cops everywhere. Then, in the distance, as I crossed College Street, I caught sight of the first of the large G20 protests. Thousands of peaceful protesters were marching, beating drums, and chanting.

A young mother stood beside me with her little son, who looked about seven years old. He appeared to be terrified. The woman saw that I was trying to make my way through the crowd to the other side of College and asked if I could put her son on my shoulders. I lifted him up and told him everything was going to be fine as we pushed into the protesters. A sympathetic group of demonstrators from a maternal rights group helped us get through. A riot cop then moved aside and put his hand on my back to urge me through, as well. Once on the other side of College there was nothing but deserted Yonge Street ahead of us. I put the boy down.

"Is the army in McDonald's?" he asked.

I told him they weren't, that it was just here and he was completely safe now.

At the Royal York that Friday things were getting crazier, as well. G8 big shots were arriving from their overnighter in Muskoka, and G20 dignitaries began rolling in, too. Down in the pool, thuggish Russian representatives came in and demanded that the table in the men's massage room be disassembled and taken up to their president's suite. The person at the health club desk explained he didn't have the authority to make such structural changes to the club on the say-so of a guest. The thugs left quickly in a huff. Later that day a number of Russian women "delegates" filed into the hotel, arms loaded down with bags from Holt Renfrew and Nine West. Clearly, it was hard work being a G20 delegate. You had to solve all the weighty problems of the world one shopping trip at a time.

By the time Saturday arrived, all of us inside the Royal York had gotten somewhat used to the routine, the ultra-paranoid security measures, and the suspension of basic freedoms. I chatted with one of the doormen, who said, "It's like the city is under siege, but it's being done to us by our own guys." Saturday had a different feeling; something was looming, and a protest that was promising to be large and contentious was drawing near. None of us had any idea just how violent and ugly that day and the next would be.

On Saturday while I was standing at the elevator in my Toronto FC shorts and Real Madrid shirt, snipers with their weapons slung over their shoulders strutted by as if their attire were no more extraordinary than mine. In my suite after my swim I showered off the chlorine, then rushed down for a coffee and breakfast sandwich at Tim Hortons. I wanted to get back to watch the Germany/England World Cup game. After the match, a 4–1 massacre of England by Germany, I decided to hustle up to Queen's Park to see first-hand what the early part of the big protest demonstration looked and felt like.

By the time I got to the park, the crowd was in the thousands, and there were just as many police on foot, on bikes, in unmarked vehicles, and in riot gear. I wandered around to check out the various causes being represented. Some were legitimate and specific, others outlandish and childish. I decided to stick close to a contingent from the United Steelworkers. The union was well organized and was marching with a little white blimp identified with its insignia. In contrast there were ominous shit-disturbers referred to as black bloc groups. The peaceful demonstrators didn't want their messages overwhelmed by the violent action of these anarchists, and the Steelworkers constantly shouted that those who chose to cover their faces couldn't march with them.

As the protest march headed south, matters got extremely tense, then violent. When water bottles filled with God knows what and golf balls started flying at cops and media vehicles, I decided it was time to head east, then south to the Royal York, away from the seething thousands. I had no idea other black bloc teams were attacking in several other city locations simultaneously. When I trotted away from the crowd, I was immediately grabbed by a police officer who demanded to see my identification. Quickly, I showed him my security clearance card and explained about living in the Royal York.

"Don't be an idiot," he said. "Get back down there behind the fence."

I told him that was exactly what I was going to do. By the time I got close to the fence and the Royal York, though, an angry, crazy mob of several hundred protesters had gathered, bent on challenging the security of the perimeter. I had to make my way through these demonstrators without appearing that I was joining them. While I watched, black bloc troublemakers operated a few feet from me. A fellow wearing a checkered shirt was surrounded by other nondescript protesters, then he fished out a black hoodie from his backpack. He put it on, donned a black balaclava, and produced a hammer. Darting out of the crowd, he hit the window of a bank several times with the hammer at what appeared to be precisely chosen points. When the glass shattered, the guy rushed back into the crowd and disappeared.

As I walked toward the King Street entry point of the security fence, I passed a police car abandoned on the street. Black bloc activists had already smashed the headlights. When I approached the fence, cops pointed at me from behind it and told me to stay away from the fence. I shouted over the hub-bub that I had a security pass and pulled it partially out of my pocket so they could see it. The fence was opened, and a Calgary policewoman grabbed me by the arm and pulled me through. She then held me against the fence until my security card was checked. Now I'm tall and weigh a pretty solid 205 pounds, but this slightly built female cop who was at least half a foot shorter than I am held me against that fence with a force I couldn't have shaken off even if I tried. I was released in short order, and the policewoman patted me on the back and apolo-gized as I headed toward the Royal York. By the time I was back in my suite, the abandoned police car I'd passed on my journey was in flames. Four other police cars were burning in various parts of the city, and an estimated 200 businesses big and small in three different areas had been trashed.

Since I had tickets to the Toronto FC/Los Angeles Galaxy soccer game at BMO Field on the Canadian National Exhibition grounds that Saturday night and I planned to go, I knew I had to walk to the stadium because all the streets were closed and pub-lic transit in the area had been halted. Even shopping malls and hospitals were on lockdown. I was determined to get away from the madness even for a couple of hours. While Harper and his party pals were getting ready to enjoy a state dinner at the Royal York, dining on Executive Chef David Garcelon's Canadian beef and local produce, I would be watching a soccer match. I called Rhonda and asked if she wanted to join me, telling her we would have to meet at the stadium because the rioting had com-pletely shut down all movement in the area. But that plan was dashed when she checked online and discovered there was no way she could get from her home in Pickering to BMO Field in any reasonable amount of time because Toronto was hunkered under a large sign that said KEEP OUT.

From what I saw on the live television coverage of the mayhem, it seemed the rioting wasn't in areas between the Royal York and BMO Field, so I ventured out two hours before kickoff. I wasn't allowed through the fence on York Street because it was sealed, so I travelled west and discovered an access point near the convention centre. As I made my way toward the second fence to find an exit out of the Red Zone, some sort of order was given to the hundreds of Calgary cops protecting the area between the two fences and suddenly the police began putting on gas masks and helmets. I approached one of the cops and told him I wanted out of the fence. He said under no circumstances was that going to happen. The fence was shut down. I said, "If I can't get out of this area and I can't get back in through the inner fence because that's sealed, could someone at least give me a gas mask to use?"

At that point out of nowhere a small knot of protesters massed to confront the police. One of the Calgary cops took me by the arm, shielded me with his body, and walked me to the wall of the nearest building, then toward an RCMP-guarded inner fence opening where I was let back through by the Mounties. Once inside the safety of the inner fence at the York Street entrance of the Royal York, there was calm again. I showed my soccer tickets to one of the RCMP officers I'd seen on a regular basis during the week and told him I was supposed to go to the game.

He chuckled. "I'd say that was rather poor planning on your part, don't you?"

I returned to my suite after being searched and paraded through a metal detector for the umpteenth time and was pretty much confined to my room for the evening while all 20 of the G20 leaders dined a few floors below me. Machine-gun-toting tactical response guys patrolled each floor, and it was suggested

that it might be better if I limited my movements in and out. I told
one commando, "There's a World Cup game on television and I
have a full bottle of cognac. Why would I want to go anywhere?"
He laughed and said he might stop by and join me for a drink.

Sunday brought even more peculiarity and horror. Harper's
festival was almost over, and everyone in the city held their collective breath, hoping things would finally calm down and their
civil rights and home would be returned to them. When I went
down to the hotel pool as usual that morning, one of the G20
leaders, the president of a European nation, was swimming. The
president's bodyguard never took his eyes off me for a second as
I swam laps with his leader, who kicked me twice in the water,
saying, "Excuse me," both times.

After my swim, I left the hotel to do my weekly half-hour on
the radio show *Bynon's Toronto Weekend* to talk about the madness the G20 Summit had brought upon the city. Strolling up
Yonge Street, I witnessed the destruction the rioters had caused
the day before. Many businesses had their windows smashed,
and in some cases stock had been thrown into the street.

As soon as I finished the radio show, I headed back to the
Royal York. Walking south toward Bay and King Streets, I came
across an army of black-clad cops and a crowd of protesters not
far from the Red Zone fence. I asked the nearest policeman what
was going on. "I don't think it's anything violent *yet*," he said.

When I got to Bay and King, the mob was noisy but contained. I knew I'd never get to the fence through all these people,
so I detoured west on King. Another solid line of riot cops closed
off the street about halfway down the block, but no other people
were there, only a line of riot cops in the distance. I took out my
security card and marched toward the roadblock, hands in the
air. As I approached, they shouted, "Stay where you are! Don't
come any closer!"

With the security card in my hand, I called back that I had clearance, was allowed inside the fence, and was trying to get to York and Wellington Streets. The police continued to warn me not to take another step forward, even though I hadn't moved since they'd told me to halt. I insisted that I wasn't a demonstrator and had clearance. At that point I was seized from behind by a big, young riot cop. He pinned me against an unmarked police SUV, then grabbed the hand holding my security card and my other hand and secured them with plastic handcuffs. Spinning me roughly, he flattened me against the vehicle and held me with a black-gloved hand.

"You were fucking warned," he growled.

I replied that I had fully complied with the warnings. He then told me I was being charged with "failure to obey ... something," or some such nonsense.

A small group of protesters watched what was happening to me and yelled, "Let him go!" At that moment I wasn't afraid. I was still thinking like a Canadian. I had done nothing wrong, so I wouldn't be arrested without grounds. Then fear crept in when I realized I wasn't in the Canada I was familiar with. Instead I was in Stephen Harper's new Canada, and mass arrests of people were occurring all around me simply because they had the nerve to get anywhere near the prime minister's private party.

While I gritted my teeth with the pain the cuffs were causing in my wrists, an older riot cop trotted over to us and asked, "What are you waving around?"

I told him I lived in the Royal York Hotel and had clearance to be inside the fence. Then I turned to show him the security card that was still in one of my cuffed hands. He took the card, studied it, frowned at the younger officer, and told him to release me.

The younger officer produced a wicked black knife from his gear and snapped the blade open. "Turn around, sir, and hold still."

I did as he said and was cut out of the cuffs. The older officer took me by the arm and walked me to the police line, telling them to clear the way so I could pass through. As the line parted, I heard the same small group of demonstrators who had protested my being handcuffed yell, "Why are you allowing him through?"

The older cop told me to walk toward York Street and not to stop. Quickly, I hustled to the RCMP-guarded fence outside the Royal York and never looked back.

That Sunday night was one of the ugliest evenings in Toronto's history. Riot cops surrounded hundreds of people, most of whom weren't protesters. In fact, many of the people out on the street thought the G20 fat cats had already left the city, and some had. The riot police employed a tactic called "kettling," in which they massed in large numbers to herd and corral people like livestock. A few hundred people were detained in this manner for several hours during a rainstorm at the intersection of Queen Street and Spadina Avenue. It was a terrifying display of state-sanctioned cruelty utterly alien to Toronto. Perhaps Harper was taking a page out of Captain William Bligh's book. Bligh, whose cruelty and uncivil treatment of his crew inspired the infamous mutiny on the *Bounty*, once said: "Cruelty with purpose is not cruelty; it's efficiency."

With the G20 Summit finally over, the Royal York quickly returned to a semblance of normality. The street cops stuck around for another day while the security apparatus was dismantled, but they all appeared to be jovial now that the weekend of carnage was becoming a memory.

On Monday, when I left the hotel, I passed some cops I'd become quite familiar with. One, a policewoman, smiled and said, "Yep, we're still here."

I smiled back. "I see that. When are you going home so we can have our freedom and dignity back?"

They all laughed, and one asked, "You aren't going to call us fascists, are you?"

"No," I replied. "But since you've used that word, I have to admit that's what you looked and sounded like."

Later that week, on the first weekend in July, Queen Elizabeth II stopped in Toronto during her Canadian visit. Where Prime Minister Harper's party of international big shots brought a plague of armed-to-the-teeth police to the city, the queen's sojourn allowed us to show visitors the good things about Canada and Canadians. Yes, there was another influx of cops and security people, but not anywhere in the numbers seen during the G20 Summit. Instead of black-clad riot police, this time law enforcement was represented only by uniformed RCMP and Toronto police officers.

At the Royal York the weekend of the queen's stopover was special for a couple of other reasons. The hotel played host not only to Her Highness but also to the annual Shriners convention. About a thousand Shriners, many of them from the U.S. South, swarmed the hotel in fezzes and colourfully decorated shirts. I had always admired the Shriners' charitable work for hospitals and sick children, and was now delighted to see them whooping it up in their mini-cars. That weekend also featured the annual Pride Parade on Sunday, which meant the Royal York was packed with royal watchers, Shriners, and gay people happily co-existing.

On Sunday morning, as I strode through the hotel lobby, I noticed a lot of people gathered in the lobby and the mezzanine lounge, then remembered that the queen was scheduled to attend a service at the nearby Cathedral Church of St. James. So I figured the crowd was waiting to catch a look at her as she left the hotel.

I exited by the Royal York's front door and found myself surrounded by RCMP officers in full dress parade reds. "I hope this isn't all for me," I joked with one.

She smiled. "Sorry, not this time."

I decided to hang around outside the velvet rope (not an imposing metal fence) for a glimpse of the queen. Standing between two Ontario Provincial Police officers, I swapped G20 horror stories with them, then watched as the royal motorcade pulled up. The queen and Prince Philip's transportation was a standard-size town car, not the armoured stretch paranoia-mobile in common use during the summit. The only marking the vehicle possessed was a small flag on the hood emblazoned with the royal coat of arms.

The queen's security guys came out to check everything, doing so efficiently and unobtrusively. As soon as they gave the okay, the red carpet was rolled out and the Mounties stood at attention. Finally, the queen emerged from the hotel with Prince Philip behind her. A bouquet of flowers in one hand, the queen smiled and waved at the crowd, then climbed into the car. As the motorcade moved off, she looked directly at the two OPP officers and me, smiled, and waved. All three of us returned the wave as if we were ecstatic children. It was a magical moment that restored the reputation and spirit of Toronto and Torontonians and helped assuage the ugly memories of the previous weekend.

Later that exceptionally hot Sunday the Pride Parade helped even more to heal the populace of a besieged city. As per usual, a million people lined Yonge Street, but this time the police patrolling the route weren't booed or jeered at. In fact, they were often applauded and patted on the back. Many even posed for pictures with paraders. Some cops donned colourful necklaces around their necks and tucked little rainbow pride flags in their gear. Several Ontario police forces actually had floats, and I had to hand it to them. It took real courage for officers to put themselves out like that in public after the behaviour of so many of their colleagues the previous weekend. The sight was wonderful to behold — a kind of reconciliation, as if the revellers were telling the police they knew the politicians were the real culprits responsible for the craziness during the summit.

Monday, July 5, marked Queen Elizabeth's state dinner at the Royal York. She was scheduled to leave the next day for New York City to address the United Nations for the first time since 1957. It was an extremely torrid day, with a humidex rating that made the temperature feel well over 40 degrees Celsius. I wrote all afternoon until about 4:30 when I packed it in. Rhonda was due to come over with a pizza soon. Then the power failed. A transformer had caught fire nearby and cut the electricity not just to the Royal York but to a large portion of downtown Toronto during rush hour on the hottest day of the year.

Downstairs Prince Philip was hosting a gathering of young people and their families who were receiving special youth achievement awards. When the room went dark, the prince, as usual, rolled with the punches and made jokes about the incident until the lights came back on. Lucky for Philip, there was emergency power for this room; the rest of the hotel was without electricity for a couple of hours. There was very little jocularity in the cavernous kitchen where the state dinner was being prepared under the expert hand of Executive Chef David Garcelon. In less than two hours the queen, Prince Philip, Prime Minister Harper, and 375 invited guests would be arriving for dinner.

Having met and conversed with Chef Garcelon a number of times, I know what a cool customer he is. He isn't the sort who shows signs of panic no matter what the problem is. However, the power failure did worry him. His reaction to the crisis, though, was instantaneous and ingenious.

Garcelon has a fortunate connection in the nearby chefs' training school at George Brown College — his wife, who is an instructor there! So he called her and arranged for the food to be transported to the school's kitchens, prepared there, and then rushed back to the hotel to be put on plates. The hotel got a delivery person to volunteer his cube van to ferry ingredients back and forth, and since there were police all over the place, a couple pitched in to escort the van through the streets to make sure no time was wasted.

To the uninitiated, the dinner went off without a hitch. Those attending had no idea what was happening behind the scenes. Everyone was treated to Garcelon's magnificent beef tenderloin, a curried mushroom risotto, and locally grown vegetables. It wasn't until the next day when the queen was about to leave the hotel for New York that it was mentioned to her that there had been a bit of drama before the dinner.

With the G20 Summit, the queen's visit, the Pride Parade, and the Shriners convention behind me, it was time to get back to the sheer enjoyment of the World Cup in South Africa. One of the most memorable games was the match that saw Spain defeat Germany 1–0, which propelled the former toward its first-ever World Cup triumph.

As a lifelong supporter of Spain, I'd worn that country's shirt throughout the tournament, even down to the hotel's health club. On the morning of Spain's great victory, a family from Germany was using the pool and the hot tub. Of course, the husband and son wore Germany shirts. They immediately noticed the Spain shirt I was sporting and smiled. I swam my laps, and the Germans continued to enjoy the hotel's amenities. Eventually, we got together around the hot tub for a discussion about the upcoming game. I told them it was the contest against Germany that I feared most. We agreed to meet for a late lunch in the EPIC lounge to watch the match.

My new German friends were as tense as I was when the game began. For a long time the two clubs were locked in a scoreless tie. There were opportunities on both sides, then Spanish veteran Carlos Puyol headed the ball into the back of the German goal. The German family collectively groaned, their excitement and cheering rapidly replaced with desperation.

Anxiously, I watched the time tick down, hoping the German team wouldn't tie things up. When the final whistle blew, I sank back in my chair with relief. My new German friends seemed stunned. When they left to pay a visit to the CN Tower, I sat back to revel in the post-game coverage.

The next major event to impact the Royal York and Toronto that summer was the annual Caribana Festival, modelled after Carnival in Trinidad, a traditional celebration first created to mark the end of the sugar cane harvest. The festival lasts for two weeks in late July and early August, culminating in a giant parade featuring steel bands and outlandish costumes.

Knowing what Caribana entailed, I expected the Royal York to be a bit noisier and crazier than usual. On that score I wasn't disappointed. It was commonplace to see people wandering the halls with glasses of rum in their hands as they drifted from one suite to another where parties were going on and Caribbean music blasted the halls. The whole affair gave the hotel a sense of something strange and magnificent taking place.

On Saturday morning, young women in their costumes, which mostly consisted of giant headpieces, a rainbow of feathers and beads, and the skimpiest of body coverings, assembled in the lobby and rode the elevators as if they were treating other guests to an advance peek at the parade that would soon occur.

The non-stop partying kept security and health club staffers on their toes for days, and the number of calls to the front desk to complain about loud music and voices soon reached record levels. But it was all great fun.

The events I witnessed during that tumultuous summer in 2010 might never be topped, but my adventure in the Royal York is ongoing, the productivity and energy boost I've enjoyed persist unabated, and the hotel will continue to stand as a beacon of grace, comfort, and class for another 80 years or more. Even though the hotel landscape of Toronto changes constantly and new hotels are rising everywhere — a Ritz-Carlton there, a Trump Hotel here, a Shangri-La Hotel there — none have the history and ambience *my* hotel possesses.

If I have to sum up my experience living in the Royal York, only one word suffices: *magical.*

(Courtesy Fairmont Hotels & Resorts)

Every year more glass-and-concrete towers rise around the Royal York, but more than 80 years after it first opened its doors the hotel still presides regally over Front Street.

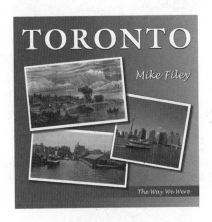

TORONTO
The Way We Were
by Mike Filey
978-1-55002-842-3
$45.00

For decades Mike Filey has regaled readers with stories of Toronto's past through its cultural landmarks and defining moments as Canada's largest city. Now, in one lavishly illustrated volume, he serves up the best of his meditations on the historical places that serve as icons of the city, the disastrous and victorious events that have shaped the metropolis, and the characters of the past and present who define it. Take Filey's personal tour of Toronto and experience the city as you never have before.

UNBUILT TORONTO

A History of the City That Might Have Been
by Mark Osbaldeston
978-1-55002-835-5
$26.99

Featuring 147 photographs and illustrations, many never before published, *Unbuilt Toronto* explores the most fascinating, never-realized building projects in and around Toronto, from the city's beginnings in the late 18th century to the 21st century. Marvel at the ambition behind some projects (early city plans that would have resulted in a Paris-by-the-Lake), be thankful for the disappearance of others (a highway through the Annex), and lament the loss of the downtown that could have been (with underground roads and walkways in the sky). Get ready to tear down your misconceptions as *Unbuilt Toronto* reintroduces you to a city you thought you knew.

Available at your favourite bookseller.

www.dundurn.com

What did you think of this book?
Visit *www.dundurn.com* for reviews, videos, updates, and more!